How to Use

History Pockets

I n *History Pockets—Ancient Egypt,* students take a travel adventure back to the time of pharaohs, mummies, and hieroglyphs. The engaging activities are stored in labeled pockets and bound into a decorative cover. Students will be proud to see their accumulated projects presented all together. At the end of the book, evaluation sheets have been added for teacher use.

Make a Pocket

1. Use a 12" x 18" (30.5 x 45.5 cm) piece of construction paper for each pocket. Fold up 6" (15 cm) to make a 12" (30.5 cm) square.

2. Staple the right side of each pocket closed.

3. Punch two or three holes in the left side of each pocket.

Assemble the Pocket Book

1. Reproduce the cover illustration on page 3 for each student.

2. Direct students to color and cut out the illustration and glue it onto a 12" (30.5 cm) square of construction paper to make the cover.

3. Punch two or three holes in the left side of the cover.

4. Fasten the cover and the pockets together. You might use string, ribbon, twine, raffia, or binder rings.

Every Pocket Has...

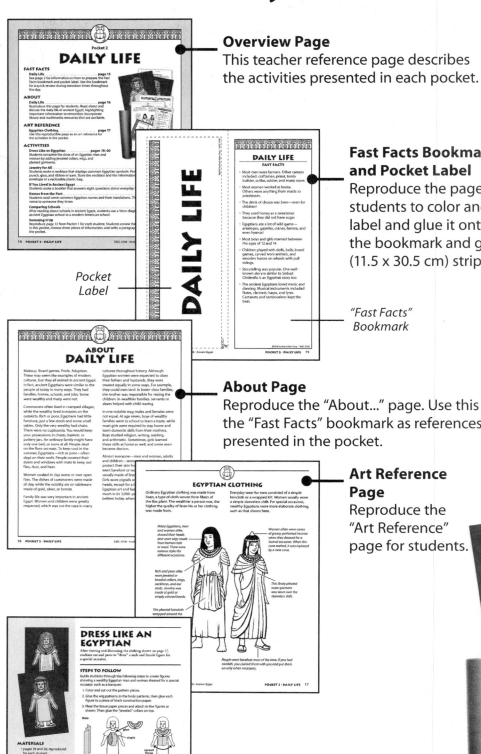

Overview Page
This teacher reference page describes the activities presented in each pocket.

Pocket Label

Fast Facts Bookmark and Pocket Label
Reproduce the page for students. Direct students to color and cut out the pocket label and glue it onto the pocket. Cut out the bookmark and glue it to a 4½" by 12" (11.5 x 30.5 cm) strip of construction paper.

"Fast Facts" Bookmark

About Page
Reproduce the "About..." page. Use this information and the "Fast Facts" bookmark as references for the activities presented in the pocket.

Art Reference Page
Reproduce the "Art Reference" page for students.

Activities
Have students do the activities and store them in the labeled pocket.

EMC 3706 • Ancient Egypt • ©2003 by Evan-Moor Corp.

ANCIENT EGYPT

NAME: _____

Pocket 1 • INTRODUCTION TO

ANCIENT EGYPT

FAST FACTS

Ancient Egypt . . . . **page 5**
See page 2 for information on how to prepare the Fast Facts bookmark and pocket label. Use the bookmark for a quick review during transition times throughout the day.

ABOUT

Ancient Egypt . . . . **page 6**
Reproduce this page for students. Read and discuss the introduction to ancient Egypt, highlighting important information to remember. Incorporate library and multimedia resources that are available.

ART REFERENCE

Ancient Egypt . . . . **page 7**
Use this map as a reference for the activities throughout the unit.

ACTIVITIES

Ancient Egypt Time Line . . . . **pages 8 & 9**
Students put together a time line showing important dates and events in ancient Egypt. Refer to this time line periodically throughout the unit.

Along the Nile . . . . **pages 10–12**
Students read about the importance of the Nile to all aspects of life in ancient Egypt. They create a fold-up booklet that shows activities along the Nile.

Summing It Up . . . . **page 13**
Reproduce page 13 for each student. Students review the information learned in this pocket, choose three pieces of information, and write a paragraph as a summary of the pocket.

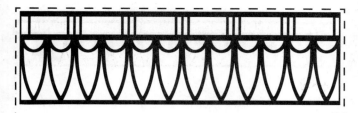

INTRODUCTION TO **ANCIENT EGYPT**

©2003 by Evan-Moor Corp. • EMC 3706

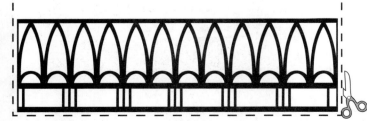

ANCIENT EGYPT
FAST FACTS

- The kingdom of ancient Egypt lasted almost 3,000 years.

- Historians divide the history of ancient Egypt into several long periods—Old Kingdom, Middle Kingdom, and New Kingdom—with shorter periods of civil war and invasion in between.

- One ancient name for Egypt was *Kemet,* meaning "black land," because of the rich black soil along the Nile River.

- The original capital of ancient Egypt was Memphis, located near the site of present-day Cairo, Egypt's current capital.

- Some historians think Menes, the first pharaoh of Egypt, built Memphis.

- During the New Kingdom, Egypt grew enormously rich by trading in gold and controlling Asian mines.

- The New Kingdom ended when, under weak rulers, one enemy after another attacked Egypt. The Nubians, Assyrians, Persians, Greeks, and Romans all controlled Egypt for a time.

- The total population of ancient Egypt was probably about 4 million.

Many more fast facts on pharaohs, pyramids, mummies, and hieroglyphs are coming up!

ABOUT ANCIENT EGYPT

The period known as ancient Egypt ended over 2,000 years ago, and it has fascinated people ever since. In fact, you may already know more about ancient Egypt than you realize—mummies, hieroglyphics, pharaohs, pyramids, papyrus, Sphinx, Cleopatra…do any of those words sound familiar?

Ancient Egypt was one of the earliest civilizations in the world, located along the mighty Nile River in what is now northern Africa. It was originally two kingdoms—Upper Egypt and Lower Egypt. At the time, the people did not use the word *Nile* or even the word *Egypt*. According to historians, ancient Egyptians called their home "Two Lands."

The rulers came to be known as pharaohs, or lords of the Two Lands. To ancient Egyptians, pharaohs were more than kings. They were living gods. People believed the pharaohs were so powerful that they kept the Nile River flowing. The ancient Egyptian society lasted roughly 3,000 years, and during that time the civilization was ruled by over 200 pharaohs spread throughout 31 dynasties, or political families.

Today the Sahara Desert covers much of northern Africa. However, when Egypt was young, the region around the Nile had a wetter climate. Every year the great river flooded, depositing rich soil along its banks and creating green grasslands where people grew crops and raised livestock. Egyptians relied on the river for many daily activities, including transportation, fishing, and recreation. The Nile was the Main Street, supermarket, and playground of ancient Egypt, all in one.

A statue of Ramses the Great at the temple at Abu Simbel.

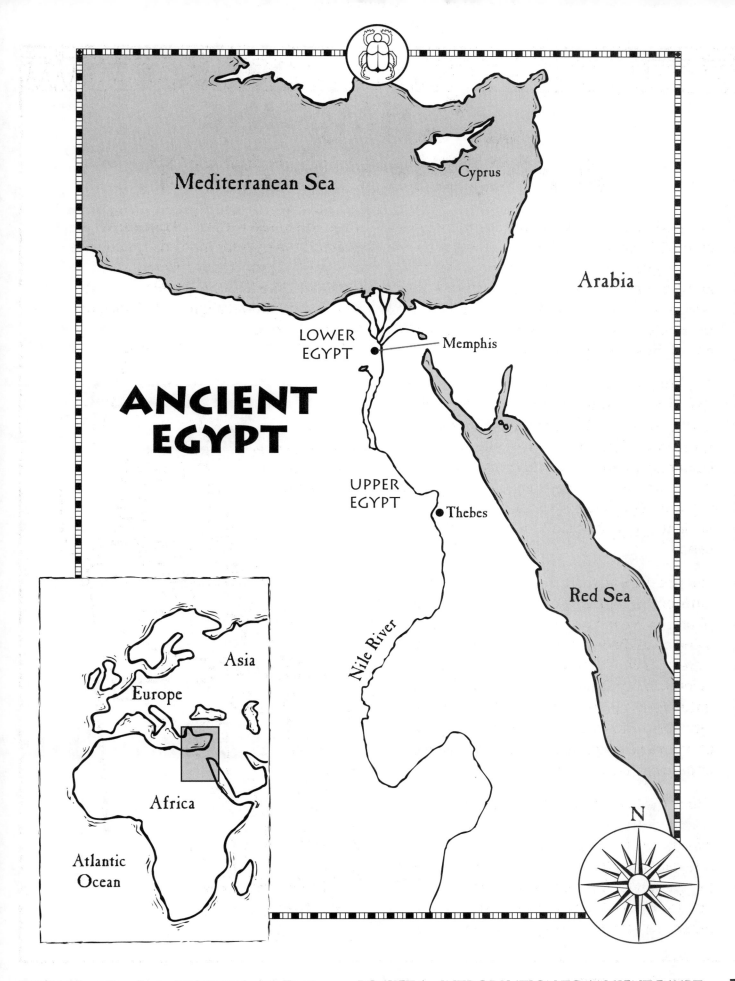

Mediterranean Sea

Cyprus

Arabia

LOWER
EGYPT •—— Memphis

ANCIENT
EGYPT

UPPER
EGYPT

• Thebes

Red Sea

Nile River

Asia

Europe

Africa

Atlantic
Ocean

N

MATERIALS

- pages 8 (bottom only) and 9, reproduced for each student
- scissors
- glue

STEPS TO FOLLOW

1. Students cut out the time line sections and glue them together.

2. As a class, read the events given on the time line. Allow students to comment on the illustrations and ask any questions that the information generates. Write student questions on a chart so that you will remember to look for answers as you proceed through the unit.

3. Fold the time line and store it in Pocket 1.

ANCIENT EGYPT TIME LINE

Students are about to travel back in time to ancient Egypt, a period of pharaonic rule and great pyramids. The period lasted from approximately 3100 B.C. to 30 B.C.

Whenever dates are given throughout the unit, refer back to this time line to help students place the events and people chronologically.

Note: The traditional abbreviations B.C. (*before Christ*) and A.D. (*anno Domini*, Latin for *in the year of the Lord*) are used throughout this book. You may choose to introduce students to the contemporary secular abbreviations of B.C.E. and C.E. as well. B.C.E. stands for *before common era*, and C.E. stands for *common era*.

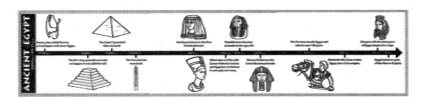

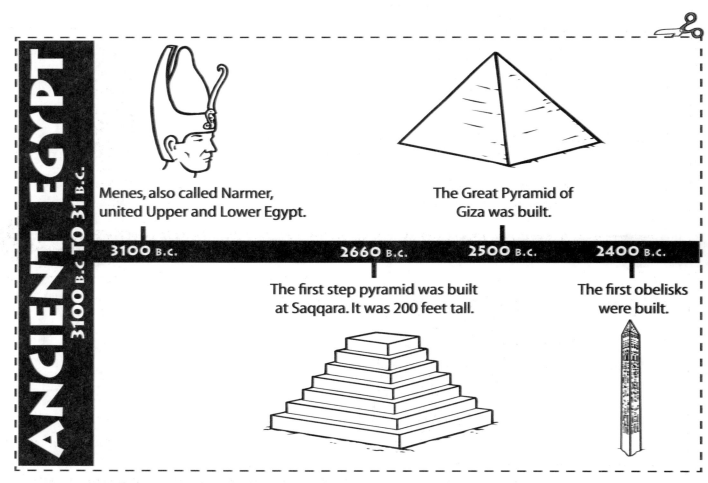

Menes, also called Narmer, united Upper and Lower Egypt.

The Great Pyramid of Giza was built.

3100 B.C.   **2660** B.C.   **2500** B.C.   **2400** B.C.

The first step pyramid was built at Saqqara. It was 200 feet tall.

The first obelisks were built.

ANCIENT EGYPT
3100 B.C. TO 31 B.C.

ANCIENT EGYPT TIME LINE

Hatshepsut became the first female pharaoh.

Tutankhamen became pharaoh at the age of 8.

1479 B.C.   **1352** B.C.   **1336** B.C.   **1279** B.C.

Akhenaten and his wife Queen Nefertiti tried to get Egyptians to believe in one god, not many.

Ramses II (Ramses the Great) became pharaoh.

Cleopatra VII, the last queen of Egypt, begins her reign.

The Persians invade Egypt and rule for over 100 years.

525 B.C.   **332** B.C.   **51** B.C.   **31** B.C.

Alexander the Great makes Egypt part of his empire.

Egypt becomes part of the Roman Empire.

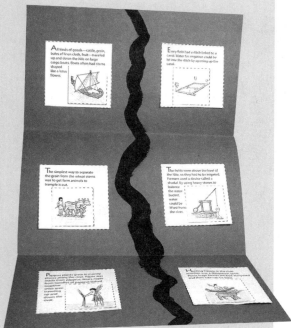

MATERIALS

- pages 11 and 12, reproduced for each student
- 10" x 18" (25.5 x 45.5 cm) tan construction paper
- blue and green tempera paint
- paintbrush
- scissors
- glue
- thin foam rubber or moleskin
- wooden block

ALONG THE NILE

The Nile was the life of Egypt. Without its floodwaters, farming would not have been possible. Students make a folded book to display information and pictures about the Nile.

STEPS TO FOLLOW

Guide students through the following steps to make their books:

1. Paint a curving "river" down the full length of the tan paper. When dry, fold in thirds as shown.

2. Read and discuss the information on the Nile presented on page 11.

3. Examine the pictures on page 11 and read the descriptions on page 12.

4. Cut out the pictures and the descriptions.

5. Glue each picture in the box with its description.

6. Glue the completed boxes along "the Nile."

7. Fold up the bottom third of the tan paper. Glue the information about the Nile from page 11 onto the flap.

8. Fold down the top third of the tan paper. Glue on the title strip.

9. Using green paint, decorate the cover with stamped papyrus flowers. (See instructions below.) When dry, add details.

PAPYRUS FLOWER STAMP

Papyrus flowers were a common symbol used in Egyptian art and architecture. Use the template provided to cut stamps from thin foam rubber. Glue the stamps onto wooden blocks. Note: Save the stamps to use with the projects on pages 22 and 69.

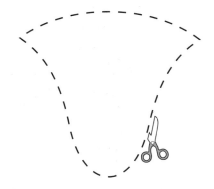

ALONG THE NILE

THE RIVER OF LIFE

The great Nile River has its beginnings in lakes far to the south of Egypt and flows more than 4,000 miles north to the Mediterranean Sea.

Life in Egypt centered on the Nile, which gave water for growing food, for drinking, and for transportation. In fact, the Egyptian calendar of three seasons was based on the yearly cycle of the Nile. The Egyptian year began in July when the floods came.

Roads could not be built on sandy desert or in places that flooded every year, so the Nile was the main road of ancient Egypt. Traveling on the Nile was easy. Going north, boats just drifted with the flow of the river. Because prevailing winds blew south, boats traveling in that direction were aided.

Each year the Nile flooded, spreading rich soil across the land. Without this annual flooding, the Egyptians could not have grown plentiful crops in the desert.

Come along on a trip on the Nile. There are wondrous sites to see.

ALONG THE NILE

The fields were above the level of the Nile, so they had to be irrigated. Farmers used a device called a shaduf. By using heavy stones to balance the water bucket, water could be lifted from the river.

glue here

The simplest way to separate the grain from the wheat stems was to get farm animals to trample it out.

glue here

Papyrus plants grew in marshy places along the river. Paper was made from papyrus. Boats made from bundles of papyrus lashed together were seen traveling up and down the river.

glue here

All kinds of goods—cattle, grain, bales of linen cloth, and fruit—were sent up and down the Nile on large cargo boats. Boats often had sterns shaped like a lotus flower.

glue here

Hunting hippos in the river marshes was a dangerous sport. These huge beasts are bad-tempered and their bite can be fatal.

glue here

Every field had a ditch linked to a canal. Water for irrigation could be let into the ditch by opening up the canal.

glue here

EMC 3706 · Ancient Egypt · ©2003 by Evan-Moor Corp.

Note: As a means of summarizing learning, reproduce this page for students to use upon the completion of each pocket.

SUMMING IT UP

Name: ______________________________

Write the title of the pocket you have just completed.

____

List three pieces of information from this pocket that you think are the most important or the most interesting.

1. ____

____

____

2. ____

____

____

3. ____

____

____

Write a paragraph with a topic sentence and the three pieces of information you chose.

____

____

____

____

____

____

____

____

____

____

Pocket 2

DAILY LIFE

FAST FACTS

See page 2 for information on how to prepare the Fast Facts bookmark and pocket label. Use the bookmark for a quick review during transition times throughout the day.

ABOUT

Reproduce this page for students. Read about and discuss the daily life of ancient Egypt, highlighting important information to remember. Incorporate library and multimedia resources that are available.

ART REFERENCE

Use this reproducible page as an art reference for the activities in the pocket.

ACTIVITIES

Students complete the dress of an Egyptian man and woman by adding jeweled collars, wigs, and pleated garments.

Students make a necklace that displays common Egyptian symbols. Provide scissors, a hole punch, glue, and ribbon or yarn. Store the necklace and the information about jewelry in an envelope or a reclosable plastic bag.

Students make a booklet that answers eight questions about everyday life in ancient Egypt.

Students read some common Egyptian names and their translations. Then they assign each name to someone they know.

After reading about schools in ancient Egypt, students use a Venn diagram to compare an ancient Egyptian school to a modern American school.

Summing It Up
Reproduce page 13 from Pocket 1 for each student. Students review the information learned in this pocket, choose three pieces of information, and write a paragraph as a summary of the pocket.

DAILY LIFE

DAILY LIFE
FAST FACTS

- Most men were farmers. Other careers included: craftsman, priest, tomb builder, scribe, soldier, and many more.

- Most women worked at home. Others were anything from maids to priestesses.

- The drink of choice was beer—even for children!

- They used honey as a sweetener because they did not have sugar.

- Egyptians ate a lot of wild game— antelopes, gazelles, cranes, herons, and even hyenas!

- Most boys and girls married between the ages of 12 and 14.

- Children played with dolls, balls, board games, carved ivory animals, and wooden horses on wheels with pull strings.

- Storytelling was very popular. One well-known story is similar to *Sinbad*. *Cinderella* is an Egyptian story too.

- The ancient Egyptians loved music and dancing. Musical instruments included flutes, clarinets, harps, and lyres. Castanets and tambourines kept the beat.

ABOUT
DAILY LIFE

Makeup. Board games. Pools. Adoption. These may seem like examples of modern cultures, but they all existed in ancient Egypt. In fact, ancient Egyptians were similar to the people of today in many ways. They had families, homes, schools, and jobs. Some were wealthy and many were not.

Commoners often lived in cramped villages, while the wealthy lived in estates on the outskirts. Rich or poor, Egyptians had little furniture, just a few stools and some small tables. Only the very wealthy had chairs. There were no cupboards. You would keep your possessions in chests, baskets, or pottery jars. An ordinary family might have only one bed, or none at all. People slept on the floor on mats. To keep cool in the summer, Egyptians—rich or poor—often slept on their roofs. People covered their doors and windows with mats to keep out flies, dust, and heat.

Women cooked in clay ovens or over open fires. The dishes of commoners were made of clay, while the nobility ate on tableware made of gold, silver, or bronze.

Family life was very important in ancient Egypt. Women and children were greatly respected, which was not the case in many cultures throughout history. Although Egyptian women were expected to obey their fathers and husbands, they were treated equally in some ways. For example, they could own land. In lower-class families, the mother was responsible for raising the children. In wealthier families, servants or slaves helped with child rearing.

In one notable way, males and females were not equal. At age seven, boys of wealthy families went to school to learn a trade, while most girls were required to stay home and learn domestic skills from their mothers. Boys studied religion, writing, reading, and arithmetic. Sometimes, girls learned these skills at home as well, and some even became doctors.

Almost everyone—men and women, adults and children—wore makeup. It helped protect their skin from the sun. Most people went barefoot or wore sandals. Clothes were usually made of linen of varying quality. Girls wore pigtails and boys had shaved heads, except for a braided tuft on one side. Egyptian art and fashion did not change much in its 3,000-year history. That is hard to believe today, when styles change often.

EMC 3706 · Ancient Egypt · ©2003 by Evan-Moor Corp.

EGYPTIAN CLOTHING

Ordinary Egyptian clothing was made from linen, a type of cloth woven from fibers of the flax plant. The wealthier a person was, the higher the quality of linen his or her clothing was made from.

Everyday wear for men consisted of a simple loincloth or a wrapped kilt. Women usually wore a simple sleeveless shift. For special occasions, wealthy Egyptians wore more elaborate clothing, such as that shown here.

Many Egyptians, men and women alike, shaved their heads and wore wigs made from human hair or wool. There were various styles for different occasions.

Rich and poor alike wore jeweled or beaded collars, rings, necklaces, and ear studs. Jewelry was made of gold or simply colored beads.

This pleated loincloth wrapped around the body and was tied in a large loop tucked in at the waist.

Women often wore cones of greasy perfumed incense when they dressed for a formal occasion. When the cone melted, it was replaced by a new cone.

This finely pleated outer garment was worn over the sleeveless shift.

People went barefoot most of the time. If you had sandals, you carried them with you and put them on only when necessary.

DRESS LIKE AN EGYPTIAN

After viewing and discussing the clothing shown on page 17, students cut and paste to "dress" a male and female figure for a special occasion.

STEPS TO FOLLOW

Guide students through the following steps to create figures showing a wealthy Egyptian man and woman dressed for a special occasion such as a banquet:

1. Color and cut out the pattern pieces.

2. Glue the wig patterns to the body patterns, then glue each figure to a piece of black construction paper.

3. Pleat the tissue paper pieces and attach to the figures as shown. Then glue the "jeweled" collars on top.

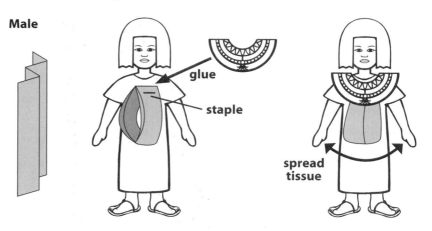

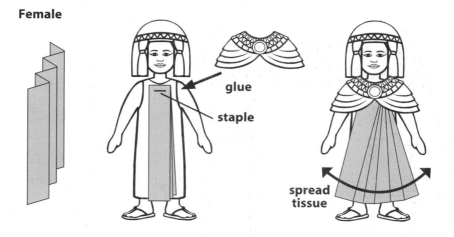

4. Instruct students to utilize information from page 17 to write a paragraph about the dress of each figure. Glue the paragraphs to the backs of the construction paper.

MATERIALS

- pages 19 and 20, reproduced for each student

- two 9" x 12" (23 x 30.5 cm) sheets of black construction paper

- white tissue paper: 5" (13 cm) square for female, 2" x 5" (5 x 13 cm) for male

- writing paper

- crayons or colored pencils

- scissors

- stapler

- glue

DRESS LIKE AN EGYPTIAN WOMAN

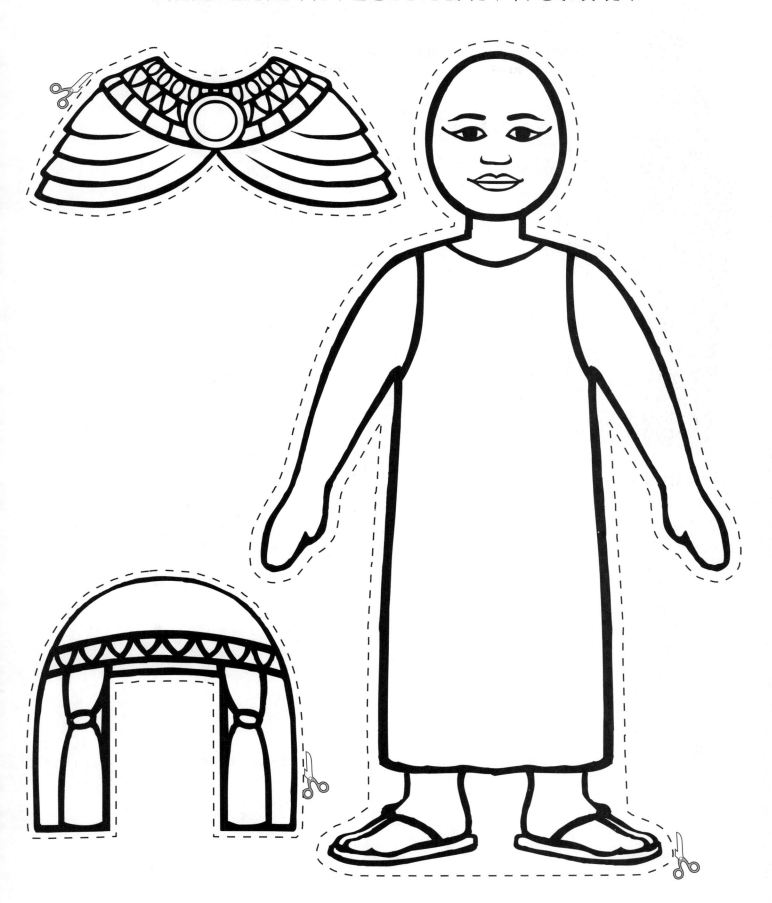

DRESS LIKE AN EGYPTIAN MAN

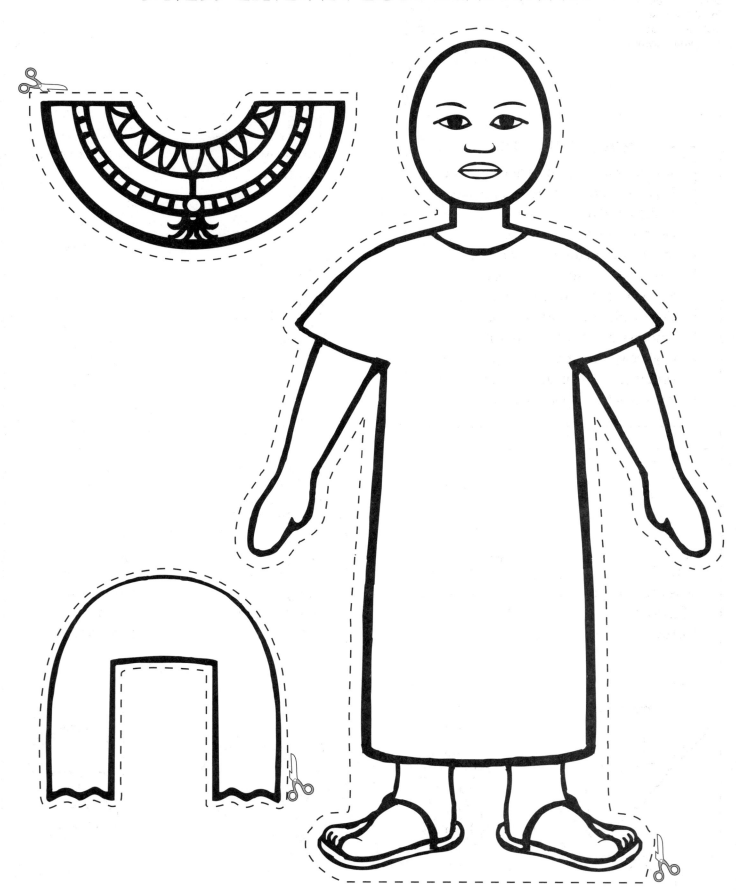

EMC 3706 · Ancient Egypt · ©2003 by Evan-Moor Corp.

Note: Reproduce this page for students to use with "Jewelry for All," as described on page 14. Make a necklace that displays all six Egyptian symbols.

JEWELRY FOR ALL

Jewelry was very popular in ancient Egypt, regardless of age, gender, or social standing. Both men and women wore earrings, necklaces, bracelets, and bands on their arms and legs. The wealthy also wore collars called wesekhs that were jeweled or beaded. Gold, lapis lazuli, turquoise, and amethysts were often used in pieces of jewelry. Even poorer Egyptians wore simple jewelry made from copper and less-valuable gemstones and ceramics.

The wedjat eye symbolized the triumph of good over evil.

— fold —

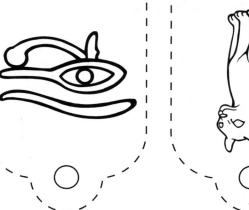

The goddess Bastet was represented by a cat.

— fold —

The falcon was the symbol of the god Horus.

— fold —

The ankh was the symbol of life.

— fold —

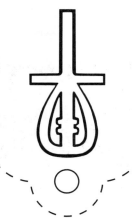

The lion was the guardian of sunrise and sunset.

— fold —

The scarab beetle was a symbol of the sun god.

— fold —

IF YOU LIVED IN ANCIENT EGYPT

One of the most interesting aspects of another culture is learning about the everyday things that people do. In this question-and-answer minibook, students read and see the answers to eight questions about life in ancient Egypt.

STEPS TO FOLLOW

Guide students through the following steps to complete the minibook:

1. Cut apart the pages of the minibook.

2. Fold on the fold lines.

   Optional: Decorate the outside flap of each page with the papyrus flower stamp. Allow the paint to dry, and then add a stem and other details to the flower.

3. Bind the pages between the two pieces of construction paper.

4. Glue on the title.

MATERIALS

- title on this page, reproduced for each student
- pages 23–26, reproduced for each student
- two 7" x 4" (18 x 10 cm) sheets of construction paper for cover
- crayons or colored pencils
- scissors
- stapler
- glue
- Optional: papyrus flower stamp (page 10) and green tempera paint

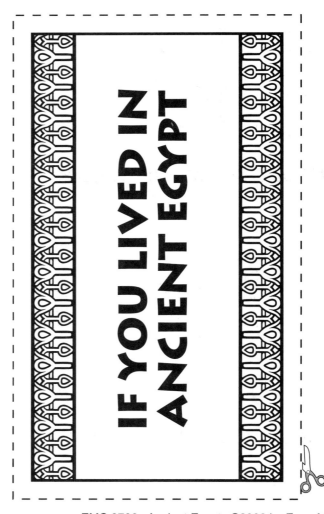

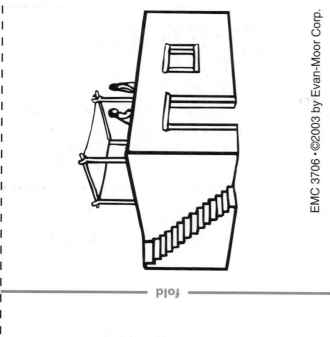

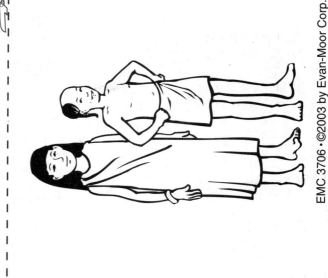

— fold —

— fold —

If your parents were working people, not rich, but not poor either, you might live in a house with several rooms. There would be a living room, a bedroom, and a kitchen. There would not be much furniture. The floors were hard-packed dirt.

When you were a little child, you did not wear clothes. The weather was warm. If you were a boy, you wore a loincloth when you got older. If you were a girl, you wore a simple dress. Clothes were made from linen, a fabric made from the flax plant.

WHERE WOULD I LIVE?

WHAT WOULD I WEAR?

staple

staple

staple

staple

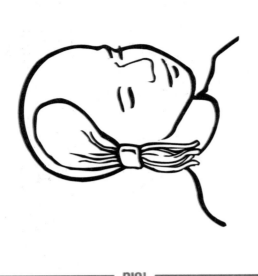

EMC 3706 · ©2003 by Evan-Moor Corp.

fold

Up to the age of 12, boys' heads were shaved except for one lock of hair on the right side of the head. This was called the lock of youth. Wealthy men and women shaved their heads and wore wigs made from wool or human hair.

WHAT KIND OF HAIRSTYLE WOULD I HAVE?

staple   staple

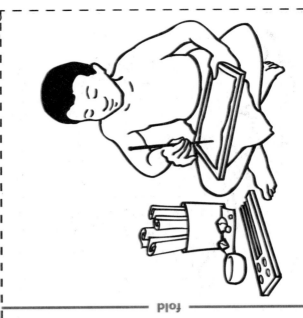

EMC 3706 · ©2003 by Evan-Moor Corp.

fold

Maybe. Peasant children helped their parents in the fields. If you were the son of a craftsman, you would learn your father's trade. Sons of wealthy families went to school to learn to be scribes or army officers. Girls stayed home to learn about homemaking from their mothers.

WOULD I GO TO SCHOOL?

staple   staple

24   POCKET 2 · DAILY LIFE

EMC 3706 · Ancient Egypt · ©2003 by Evan-Moor Corp.

fold

You would eat a lot of the same things we do today—bread, vegetables, fish, poultry, and beef. You wouldn't want to eat pork, though. It was thought to be unclean. You would eat a lot of figs and melons, but not oranges and bananas. These fruits were unknown.

Cats were the favorite pet. Rich people even had their cats mummified. If you had a dog, it probably looked a lot like a greyhound. Wealthy families might have a monkey as a pet.

EMC 3706 · ©2003 by Evan-Moor Corp.

EMC 3706 · ©2003 by Evan-Moor Corp.

WHAT FOODS WOULD I EAT?

WOULD I HAVE A PET?

staple

staple

staple

staple

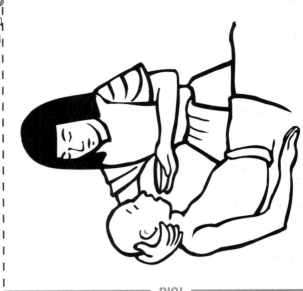

You could play catch with a clay ball filled with beads to make it rattle. There was a favorite board game called senet. Men liked to go hunting. There were festivals of the gods that sometimes lasted several days.

WHAT COULD I DO FOR FUN?

Doctors in ancient Egypt had many methods to help sick people. They knew how important diet was, and they could set broken bones.

WHAT IF I GOT SICK?

Name: _____

NAMES FROM THE PAST

Just like modern families, ancient Egyptians took great care in choosing names for their children. Egyptian names could be a single word or a group of words that formed a statement. Names could be used for either a male or a female. It was common for female names to reflect women's beauty or behavior, however. Just like today, nicknames were also used. Names could be changed for several reasons. Pharaohs changed their names to honor a new god, or commoners changed their names to honor pharaohs. Sometimes people chose new names to reflect positive events in their lives. Egyptian names, just like modern names, could go in and out of popularity.

Directions:
Read each of the ancient Egyptian names below and their meanings. Does a particular name seem to fit someone you know? Write the person's name and explain why you would give him or her that Egyptian name.

ANCIENT EGYPTIAN NAMES	TRANSLATION	NAME OF PERSON YOU KNOW	REASON FOR RENAMING
Ahmose	The Moon Is Born		
Her-uben	Resplendent Sky		
Miw-sher	Kitten		
Netikert	She Who Is Excellent		
Pasebakhaenniut	The Star That Appears in the City		
Tepemkau	Best of Souls		
Wahankh	Strong in Life		
Neferet	Pretty		

Name: _____

COMPARING SCHOOLS

Most Egyptian children did not go to school. Children started helping their parents by the age of four. Boys of artisans and farmers learned their fathers' trades. Girls were not allowed to go to school; they learned household chores from their mothers. However, there is evidence that royal children were taught reading, writing, and mathematics in the palace. Only boys of wealthy parents were allowed to join temple schools to become scribes or army officers.

Boys who attended these schools to become scribes started at age four or five. The boys had very strict teachers who could hit them on their backs with a rod. The boys had to read and write 700 hieroglyphs by heart. They used reed pens to copy the hieroglyphs onto pieces of broken pottery. The boys were not allowed to practice on valuable papyrus. The students spent part of the day chanting texts aloud. The boys also studied math, law, history, and geography. Some also learned astronomy, engineering, and architecture. There was no time in the day for recess, sports, or games. If the boys made it through seven years of this demanding school, they were rewarded with a good job at the temple or in the royal court.

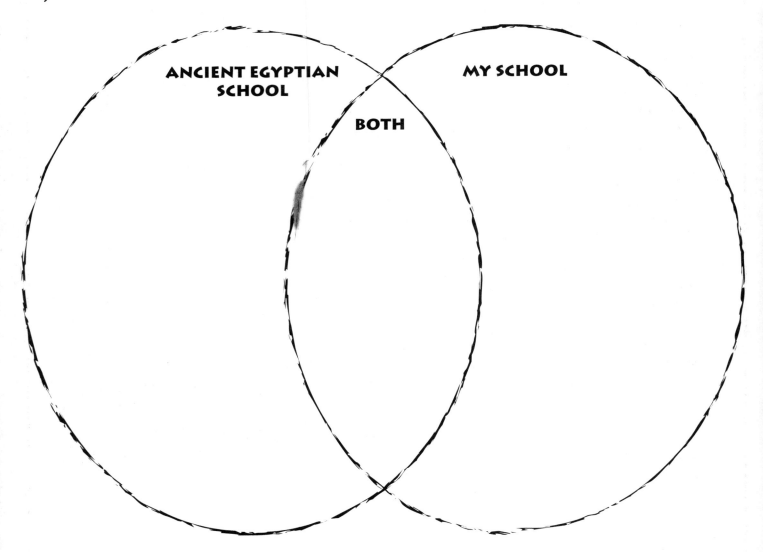

ANCIENT EGYPTIAN SCHOOL

MY SCHOOL

BOTH

EMC 3706 · Ancient Egypt · ©2003 by Evan-Moor Corp.

GOVERNMENT AND LEADERS

FAST FACTS

Government and Leaders.................... **page 30**
See page 2 for information on how to prepare the Fast Facts bookmark and pocket label. Use the bookmark for a quick review during transition times throughout the day.

ABOUT

Government and Leaders.................... **page 31**
Reproduce this page for students. Read about and discuss the government and leaders of ancient Egypt, highlighting important information to remember. Incorporate library and multimedia resources that are available.

ART REFERENCE

Pyramid of Power .... **page 32**
Use this reproducible page as a reference as you read "About Government and Leaders."

ACTIVITIES

Help Wanted .... **pages 33 & 34**
Students utilize the "Pyramid of Power" chart on page 32 and the job descriptions from the *Egyptian Times,* and then decide which job they would like to apply for (page 34). (The job of pharaoh is already taken.) When the task is completed, students glue pages 33 and 34 to either side of a piece of construction paper before storing it in the pocket.

A Gallery of Rulers .... **pages 35–43**
Students read about six pharaohs and queens, complete a crossword puzzle about them, and then bind the information into a book.

Summing It Up
Reproduce page 13 from Pocket 1 for each student. Students review the information learned in this pocket, choose three pieces of information, and write a paragraph as a summary of the pocket.

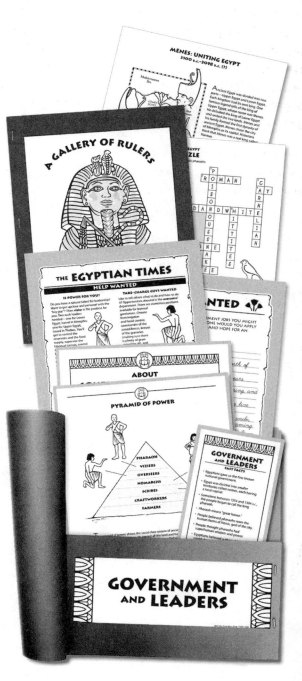

GOVERNMENT AND LEADERS

GOVERNMENT AND LEADERS

FAST FACTS

- Egyptians gave us the first known national government.

- Egypt was divided into smaller territories called nomes, each having a local capital.

- Sometime between 1554 and 1304 B.C., the people began to call the king "pharaoh."

- *Pharaoh* means "great house."

- People believed pharaohs were the human forms of Horus, god of the sky.

- People thought pharaohs had superhuman wisdom and power.

- Egyptians believed a pharaoh's crown could shoot flames.

- When a pharaoh was near, all had to kneel or lie down to show respect.

- All of Egypt belonged to the pharaoh.

- People paid taxes to the pharaoh by giving part of their crops, serving in the military, or building a monument.

- Since there was not actual money, people exchanged goods. A donkey and two pairs of sandals might equal five pieces of linen and a sack of grain.

©2003 by Evan-Moor Corp. • EMC 3706

©2003 by Evan-Moor Corp. • EMC 3706

ABOUT GOVERNMENT AND LEADERS

The world's first known national government was formed in ancient Egypt when Menes united Upper and Lower Egypt around 3100 B.C. Menes is now considered to be Egypt's first pharaoh (another word for king or ruler). He started the first dynasty, which is a group of rulers from the same family. Ancient Egypt had 31 dynasties, during which over 200 pharaohs reigned, one after the other. Some dynasties lasted for a long time, and others were fairly short.

Pharaohs were not elected by the people. They inherited their positions. Pharaohs often had more than one wife, and the oldest son of the chief wife would become the next pharaoh.

Today, the word *pharaoh* refers to all rulers of ancient Egypt. However, for much of their history, Egyptians did not call their kings pharaohs. The word did not come into use in Egypt until the Eighteenth Dynasty (sometime between 1539 and 1295 B.C.).

Government and religion were very closely connected. Egyptians believed that the pharaohs were all-powerful gods on Earth. Pharaohs were supreme rulers who issued laws, ran the army, managed the economy, and generally handled all other aspects of Egyptian society.

The pharaoh relied on advisors to help run the country. The priests took care of the country's important religious needs. High-ranking officials, called viziers and overseers, assisted the pharaoh in running the government. The officials were responsible for areas such as tax collection, royal granaries, and law courts. Each of the 42 districts in ancient Egypt had its own governor, or nomarch. The governors ran the day-to-day operations of their districts. The scribes were another important group of officials. They were ancient Egypt's writers and recordkeepers. The pharaoh and the government officials had to depend on the hardworking craftspeople and farmers to keep the country running smoothly.

People did not use bills and coins as money. Instead, they paid in goods (usually crops) and services (such as serving in the military or helping to build a monument). The pharaoh did not have a bank but rather a warehouse filled with crops that people had paid as taxes.

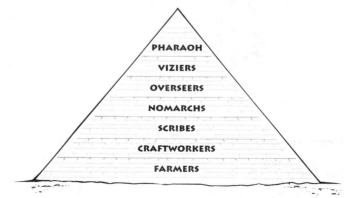

PYRAMID OF POWER

PHARAOH

VIZIERS

OVERSEERS

NOMARCHS

SCRIBES

CRAFTWORKERS

FARMERS

The pyramid of power shows the social class system of ancient Egypt. The pharaoh was the most powerful person. He owned all the land and had complete control over all of his people. He relied on high-ranking advisors called viziers to help him rule. The viziers were supported by a group of overseers. Each overseer was responsible for a particular part of the government. The nomarchs were the governors for each of the 42 districts. The scribes were the writers and recordkeepers for the country. The skilled craftworkers provided the goods for the pharaoh and his family. Farmers formed the large base of the Egyptian social pyramid.

 EMC 3706 · Ancient Egypt ·©2003 by Evan-Moor Corp.

THE EGYPTIAN TIMES

HELP WANTED

IS POWER FOR YOU?

Do you have a natural talent for leadership? Want to get upclose and personal with the "big guy"? Then **vizier** is the position for you. Two such leaders needed—one for Lower Egypt, based in Memphis; one for Upper Egypt, based in Thebes. You'll get to control the reservoirs and the food supply, supervise the biannual census, control the collection of taxes, be the head of the court system, and lots of other really top-notch stuff. Apply to the pharaoh at the palace in Thebes.

WANT TO BE A NOMARCH?

Well, OK, there are 42 jobs just like this one in the country. But you live in this nome, so why not apply? As **nomarch**, you'll get to call the shots on a whole bunch of craftworkers, farmers, and even scribes. You'll have total authority over your area and become very rich.

Send resume to:
    Vizier, Lower Egypt
    Memphis

TAKE-CHARGE GUYS WANTED

Like to tell others what to do and how to do it? Opportunities abound in the **overseers'** department. There are numerous positions available for learned gentlemen. Choose from irrigation and flood control, commander of the armed forces, keeper of the granaries (making sure there is plenty of grain stored for all), and other equally exciting positions.

JACK-OF-ALL-TRADES

The writing is on the wall. **Scribes** do it all! This is where your career path begins. Start out as a tax collector (bodyguard provided) or a scribe for the army (you may have to count the severed right hands of the enemy, so the squeamish should not apply), and work your way up. To where, you ask? Remember that all overseers, governors, and viziers are trained as scribes. Must know your hieroglyphs forward and backward. Papyrus scrolls provided.

 # HELP WANTED

YOU HAVE READ ABOUT FOUR GOVERNMENT JOBS YOU MIGHT HAVE HAD IN ANCIENT EGYPT. WHICH ONE WOULD YOU APPLY FOR? FILL OUT THE APPLICATION BELOW AND HOPE FOR AN INTERVIEW!

NAME _____

WHAT JOB ARE YOU APPLYING FOR? _____
_____

WHERE DO YOU LIVE? _____
_____

WHAT SCHOOLING HAVE YOU HAD? _____
_____
_____
_____

ARE YOU WILLING TO RELOCATE? _____
_____

LIST YOUR QUALIFICATIONS FOR THIS JOB. _____
_____
_____
_____
_____

TELL WHY YOU WOULD LIKE TO HAVE THIS JOB. _____
_____
_____
_____

   EMC 3706 · Ancient Egypt · ©2003 by Evan-Moor Corp.

A GALLERY OF RULERS

There were more than 200 pharaohs in the over 3,000-year history of ancient Egypt. Some were more memorable than others. Students read about six pharaohs and queens and create a book to showcase the information. The last page of the book is a crossword puzzle that gives students the opportunity to consolidate all the information.

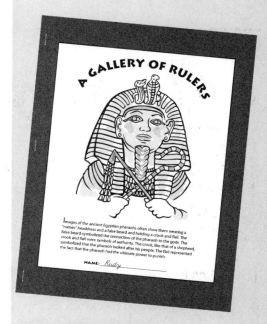

STEPS TO FOLLOW

Guide students through the following steps to make a book about some famous pharaohs:

1. Read and discuss each biography. You may wish to cover one pharaoh or queen at a time and include other information resources, such as film, videotape, books, and Internet sites.

2. Color the cover illustration on page 36. Glue it to one piece of black construction paper.

3. Bind all the information pages between the two sheets of construction paper, using staples or a hole punch and yarn.

MATERIALS

- pages 36–43, reproduced for each student
- two 9" x 12" (23 x 30.5 cm) sheets of black construction paper
- crayons or colored pencils
- scissors
- glue
- stapler or hole punch and yarn

Suggested Answers

page 37
Menes is remembered because he united Upper Egypt and Lower Egypt into one country. Menes was the first ruler to wear the double crown.

page 38
Queen Hatsheput is remembered because she was the first female ruler to act like a man and be called a pharaoh. She repaired temples and increased trade with other lands.

page 39
Nefertiti is remembered because she and her husband tried to get the people to believe in one god instead of many gods.

page 40
Ramses II is remembered because he lead the Egyptian army to victory over the Hittites. He also built more temples and monuments than any other pharaoh.

page 41
Tutankhamen is remembered because of all the treasures found in his tomb.

page 42
Cleopatra VII is remembered because she charmed and won the support of Roman rulers Julius Caesar and Marc Antony. She was the last ruler of independent Egypt.

page 43

A GALLERY OF RULERS

Images of the ancient Egyptian pharaohs often show them wearing a headdress and a false beard, and holding a crook and flail. The false beard symbolized the connection of the pharaoh to the gods. The crook and flail were symbols of authority. The crook, like that of a shepherd, symbolized that the pharaoh looked after his people. The flail represented the fact that the pharaoh had the ultimate power to punish.

NAME: _____

MENES: UNITING EGYPT
3100 B.C.–3098 B.C. (?)

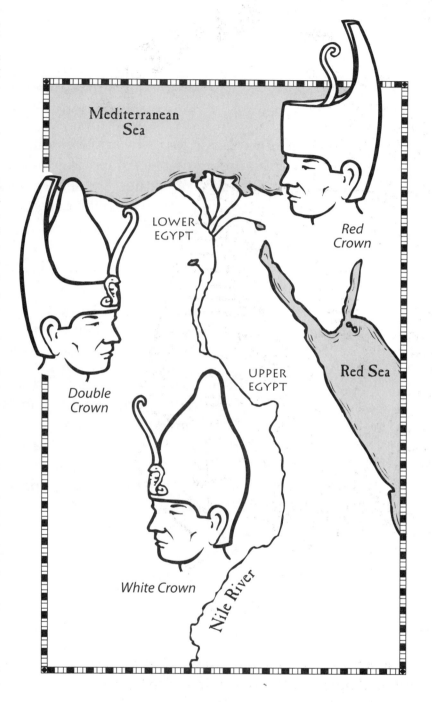

Ancient Egypt was divided into two parts—Upper Egypt and Lower Egypt. Each kingdom had its own king. One famous legend tells of the king of Upper Egypt, whose name was Menes. He defeated the king of Lower Egypt and united the two lands. Menes and his family formed the first dynasty of ancient Egypt. Menes chose the city of Memphis as its capital. Historians think that Menes was a real king called Narmer.

Menes was the first to wear the double crown. The crown of Upper Egypt was tall and white. The crown of Lower Egypt was red. The white crown was put on first and the red crown fit over and around it. Wearing both crowns symbolized the unification of Egypt.

Menes is remembered because _____

_____

_____

_____

QUEEN HATSHEPSUT: THE FIRST FEMALE PHARAOH
1479 B.C.–1457 B.C.

The hieroglyphs in this cartouche represent the name Hatshepsut.

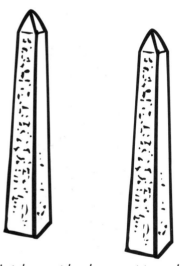

Queen Hatshepsut had a great temple and gigantic granite pillars called obelisks erected in her honor. Stonecutters carved words of praise for the queen on the obelisks.

In the Eighteenth Dynasty, Hatshepsut was willing to act like a man to be pharaoh of Egypt. She wore men's clothing and even wore a false beard. There had been female rulers in Egypt before, but none were pharaohs.

She is remembered for many achievements. Hatshepsut ordered repairs of temples that had been damaged in battles. She sent miners back to work digging for ores in the deserts. Hatshepsut increased trade too. Expeditions to Punt (present-day Somalia) were made to bring back gold, ivory, wood, leopard skins, and other exotic animals. Like the other pharaohs, she wanted to be remembered, so she ordered a temple and two obelisks to be built in her honor.

During Hatshepsut's reign, Egypt enjoyed peace and renewed prosperity. No one knows for sure what happened to her. Some think she was murdered, while others think she just retired from politics to let Thutmose III and her second daughter rule. Her body was never found. We do know that after her reign, her name and image were removed from every monument.

Queen Hatshepsut is remembered because _____

_____

_____

_____

EMC 3706 · Ancient Egypt · ©2003 by Evan-Moor Corp.

NEFERTITI: A QUEEN OF GREAT BEAUTY
1350 B.C.–1334 B.C.

Nefertiti was a queen in the Eighteenth Dynasty. She is very well known today in part because of the limestone bust of her that was found. It is currently in a German museum. Her husband, Amenhotep IV, changed his name to Akhenaten in honor of the sun god, Aten. Akhenaten and Nefertiti supported radical changes in religion. She and her husband tried to change religion from belief in many gods to only one god.

Nefertiti may have ruled Egypt for a short time after her husband's death. One of Nefertiti's daughters was the wife of Tutankhamen.

This famous bust of Nefertiti was carved from limestone and then painted.

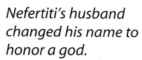
Nefertiti's husband changed his name to honor a god.

Nefertiti is remembered because_____

_____

_____

_____

POCKET 3 · GOVERNMENT AND LEADERS 39

RAMSES II: THE GREAT PHARAOH
1279 B.C.–1213 B.C.

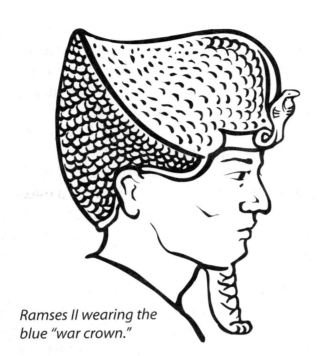

Ramses II wearing the blue "war crown."

Ramses II (also spelled Ramesses) was the only pharaoh to have the title "the Great" added to his name. Perhaps this was because he led the Egyptian army into the Middle East and defeated a force of 40,000 Hittites. Later in his reign he signed a peace treaty with the Hittites that lasted until his death. Or perhaps he was called Ramses the Great because he ordered the construction of more temples, statues, and obelisks than any other pharaoh. He is said to have had more than 100 children. Ramses II lived a long life, dying at the age of 86. Nine other pharaohs took the name Ramses in honor of him.

A golden sledge pulled the sarcophagus of Ramses II to his tomb in the Valley of the Kings.

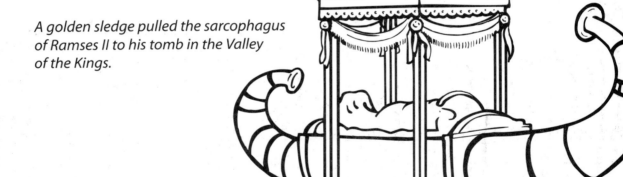

Ramses II is remembered because _____

_____

_____

_____

  EMC 3706 · Ancient Egypt · ©2003 by Evan-Moor Corp.

TUTANKHAMEN: BOY KING
1134 B.C.–1125 B.C.

Tutankhamen's death mask is probably the best-known work of art from ancient Egypt. It was made of gold inlaid with carnelian, lapis lazuli, and colored glass.

Tutankhamen was only eight or nine years old when he became pharaoh in the Eighteenth Dynasty. King Tutankhamen was a good student, but was in delicate health. He enjoyed riding, archery, swimming, and hunting much more than ruling his kingdom. Tutankhamen had two high officials who ruled with him. They were Ay, his uncle, and Horemheb, the commander-in-chief of the army. To make him appear older and wiser, his advisors had him marry when he became pharaoh. He died young, at about age 18.

Because of his young age and short reign, Tutankhamen was a relatively unimportant pharaoh. He is well known today because of the treasures found in his tomb, which was discovered relatively undamaged in 1922 in the Valley of the Kings.

Tutankhamen's mummy was placed in three coffins. This second coffin was made of wood and covered with gold and semiprecious stones. The inner coffin was solid gold.

Tutankhamen is remembered because _____

_____

_____

_____

CLEOPATRA VII: THE LAST QUEEN OF EGYPT
51 B.C.–30 B.C.

Queen Cleopatra VII was known for her ambition, charm, intelligence, and wit.

The hieroglyphs in this cartouche represent the name Cleopatra.

Cleopatra VII was the last ruler of independent Egypt and the most famous of all Egyptian queens. Her short life (69 B.C. to 30 B.C.) was full of intrigue and controversy.

Cleopatra's father, Ptolemy XII, left the throne to both his son and daughter. Cleopatra's brother had her exiled so that he could become sole ruler. When Julius Caesar, the Roman general, visited Egypt, Cleopatra convinced him to help her regain power.

Cleopatra followed Caesar back to Rome and lived there until Caesar was murdered. Fearing for her life, she returned to Egypt with her young son by Caesar. Not long after her return to Egypt, Cleopatra's brother died. Many believe that Cleopatra had him poisoned so that she and her son could become the new rulers.

Cleopatra was worried that Egypt would become a province of Rome. She went to Marc Antony, the ruler of the Eastern Roman Empire, for help. Antony let Egypt remain an independent country. The Romans did not trust Cleopatra, however, and Antony lost power.

The new ruler of Rome, Octavian, wanted to conquer Egypt. Cleopatra tried to charm him, but she did not succeed. Octavian ordered her to be taken prisoner. Rather than live like that, Cleopatra decided to end her own life. She reached into a basket containing a very poisonous snake and died shortly thereafter.

Cleopatra VII is remembered because _____

_____

_____

EMC 3706 · Ancient Egypt · ©2003 by Evan-Moor Corp.

PHARAOHS AND QUEENS OF EGYPT
CROSSWORD PUZZLE

Use the information you have read on the six pharaohs
and queens to complete the puzzle.

ACROSS

2. the empire that ruled Egypt after the death of Cleopatra
4. the official who ruled with Tutankhamen
8. the colors of the double crown (3 words)
10. Ramses II built more temples, statues, and _____ than any other pharaoh.
11. the material from which the famous bust of Nefertiti was carved
12. the number of coffins in which Tutankhamen's mummy was placed

DOWN

1. the means by which Cleopatra died (2 words)
3. a reddish stone used in Tutankhamen's death mask
5. the only pharaoh to be called "the Great"
6. the king who united Upper and Lower Egypt
7. the last queen of Egypt
9. the people defeated by Ramses

Pocket 4

RELIGION

FAST FACTS

See page 2 for information on how to prepare the Fast Facts bookmark and pocket label. Use the bookmark for a quick review during transition times throughout the day.

ABOUT

Reproduce this page for students. Read about and discuss the religion of ancient Egypt, highlighting important information to remember. Incorporate library and multimedia resources that are available.

ART REFERENCE

Use this reproducible page as a reference as you study about Egyptian religion.

ACTIVITIES

Many Egyptian gods and goddesses were human-animal hybrids. Students re-create a series of deities by making their own flip book.

Students make a book depicting how a mummy was interred and read about the steps of embalming.

The tombs of the nobility had several rooms to house the items the dead would need in the afterlife. Students place items in the correct rooms of the tomb.

Summing It Up
Reproduce page 13 from Pocket 1 for each student. Students review the information learned in this pocket, choose three pieces of information, and write a paragraph as a summary of the pocket.

EMC 3706 · Ancient Egypt · ©2003 by Evan-Moor Corp.

RELIGION

RELIGION
FAST FACTS

- In Arabic the word *mummy* means "pitch-preserved body."

- Priests had to wash several times a day and remove all hair from their bodies.

- Priests could not wear wool or sandals made of leather. These were thought to be unclean.

- High priests treated the statues of the gods like real people. They washed them, dressed them, and put makeup on them.

- Gods were believed to have human traits. They ate, had emotions, gave birth, had families, and died.

- Many Egyptians wore amulets to protect them from evil spirits.

- Women could get jobs as mourners at funerals. They were paid to wail and pull their hair.

- Prayers, hymns, and magic spells were found in the Book of the Dead, which was wrapped in the cloth of mummies to help the dead person make a smooth transition into the afterlife.

- As soon as a new king took the throne, he ordered an architect to begin working on his tomb.

- Tombs were built in the Land of the Dead, on the west side of the Nile. The work took many years to complete.

ABOUT
RELIGION

Religion was found in every aspect of ancient Egyptian society, including government, science, and art. Egyptians worshiped many deities (gods and goddesses). They believed that their deities were responsible for every action in their world, big and small—from the sunrise to a sneeze. However, ancient Egyptians did not call their belief in deities a religion. To them, the gods were simply a part of everyday life and a force of nature. On a daily basis, people showed respect to the gods, asked them for help, and feared them.

Egyptians had different types of gods, and there were many stories about each god. Some were worshiped throughout all of Egypt, such as the sun god, named Ra or Aten. Others were only known to a single nome (a division of land in ancient Egypt, similar to a town). Many gods and goddesses were depicted as a human with the head of an animal. Egyptian deities were not a set group that never changed. Some pharaohs favored certain gods. Throughout the long history of ancient Egypt, deities came and went depending on what the pharaoh of the time wanted. Sometimes more than one god was merged to form a single new god. One pharaoh, Amenhotep IV, tried to convince Egyptians to worship only one god instead of many. His idea did not last long.

Although pharaohs were human beings, the people considered them gods. Pharaohs built extravagant temples to honor themselves and the gods. Egyptians believed that the spirits of their deities lived in the temples. The temples were the center of each community. They contained sanctuaries with statues of the gods and goddesses, but only the pharaohs and high priests could enter them. Therefore, most other people prayed at home. Festivals were held to praise the gods and goddesses, especially during flood season when farmers were not able to work in the fields.

Egyptians looked forward to life after death, or the afterlife. They believed they would continue to live after they died, but in a different way than before. Because people wanted to enjoy the afterlife, they spent a great deal of time preparing their tombs for that purpose. If possible, they were buried with the comforts of life such as food, clothes, furniture, jewelry, and household items so they could use them in the afterlife. Bodies were mummified—preserved using special treatments and chemicals—so that people could use their bodies in the afterlife. The process of making a mummy is called embalming. The embalmers did such a good job, and Egypt's climate is so dry, that many mummies have survived to the present day.

EMC 3706 · Ancient Egypt · ©2003 by Evan-Moor Corp.

TEMPLES OF ANCIENT EGYPT

Temples were built as houses for the gods. It was here that the pharaoh could talk to them. Every town had its own temple dedicated to the town's gods. However, the common people could not enter the temples. Only priests, as the representatives of the pharaoh, could go in.

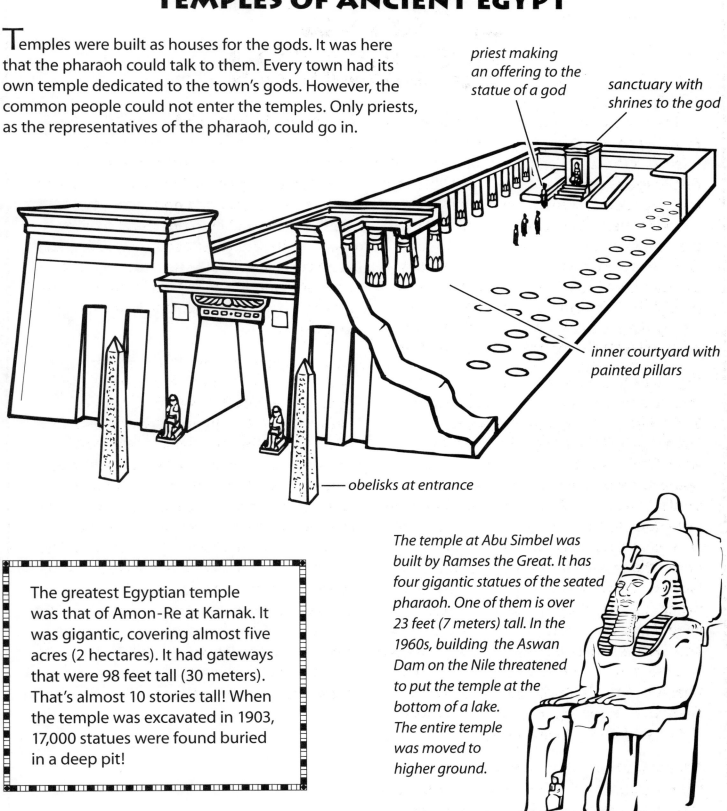

priest making an offering to the statue of a god

sanctuary with shrines to the god

inner courtyard with painted pillars

obelisks at entrance

The greatest Egyptian temple was that of Amon-Re at Karnak. It was gigantic, covering almost five acres (2 hectares). It had gateways that were 98 feet tall (30 meters). That's almost 10 stories tall! When the temple was excavated in 1903, 17,000 statues were found buried in a deep pit!

The temple at Abu Simbel was built by Ramses the Great. It has four gigantic statues of the seated pharaoh. One of them is over 23 feet (7 meters) tall. In the 1960s, building the Aswan Dam on the Nile threatened to put the temple at the bottom of a lake. The entire temple was moved to higher ground.

MATERIALS

- pages 49–51, reproduced for each student
- pencil
- crayons or colored pencils
- scissors
- stapler
- glue

A MENAGERIE OF GODS

Some ancient Egyptian gods and goddesses appeared to be fully human. Many others were shown with the bodies of humans and the heads of animals or birds. Animals, particularly cats, were sacred to ancient Egyptians. A god with the head of an animal usually had some similarity to that animal. For example, the goddess of war, Sekhmet, often had the head of a lioness to show she was fierce.

Students create a flip book of some of the gods and goddesses of ancient Egypt.

STEPS TO FOLLOW

1. Discuss information on gods and goddesses from this pocket and any additional reference materials you have collected.

2. Read the information on page 51 and match the paragraphs with the gods and goddesses depicted on pages 49 and 50.

3. Have students cut apart the flip book on pages 49 and 50. Glue the information about each god on the back of the picture, making sure to place it below the cut line on the picture.

4. Students assemble the book and staple it where indicated.

5. Students then carefully cut on the dotted lines of each page. This will create a flip-book effect.

6. The last page of the flip book is for the students to create a god or goddess. They do this by drawing a body of an Egyptian and the head of an animal of choice. They should name the god and give its purpose. On the back of the new god, they should write a description of the god's duties.

7. Students color the flip book.

8. Students will enjoy making different forms of the gods and goddesses by interchanging heads and bodies.

EMC 3706 · Ancient Egypt · ©2003 by Evan-Moor Corp.

A MENAGERIE OF GODS

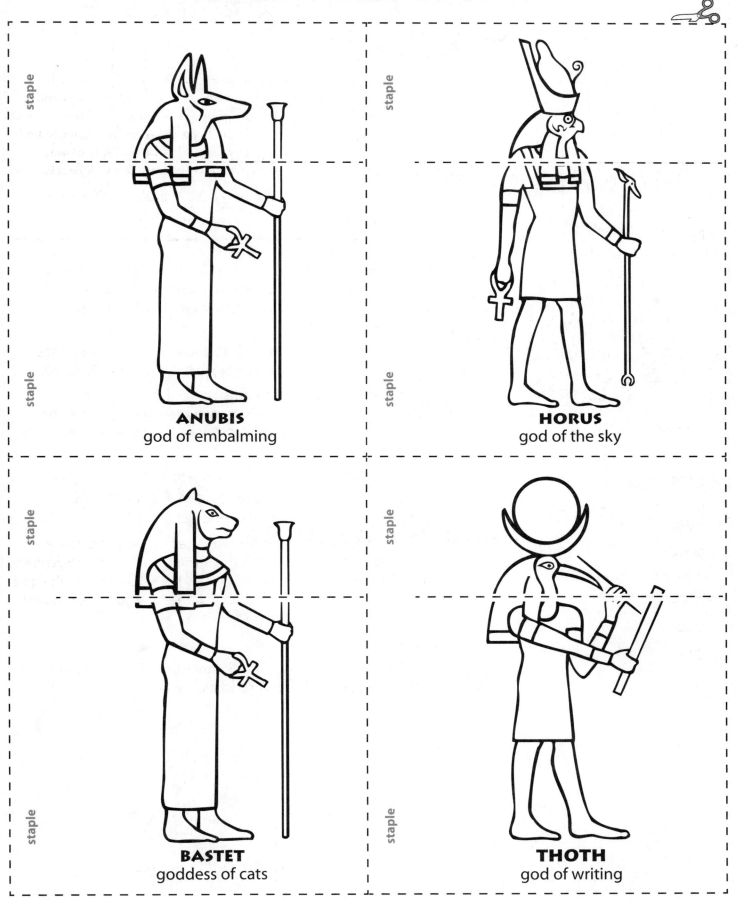

staple

staple

ANUBIS
god of embalming

staple

staple

HORUS
god of the sky

staple

staple

BASTET
goddess of cats

staple

staple

THOTH
god of writing

A MENAGERIE OF GODS

HATHOR
goddess of love

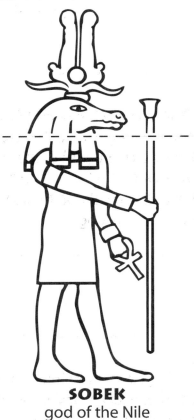

SOBEK
god of the Nile

name of god _____

god of _____

NAME _____

   EMC 3706 · Ancient Egypt · ©2003 by Evan-Moor Corp.

A MENAGERIE OF GODS

Cut out the descriptions of these Egyptian gods and glue them to the backs of the pictures.

Shown with the head of a falcon and wearing the double crown, Horus was the god of the sky. His eyes were the Sun and the Moon. It was believed that his spirit entered the king.

The goddess of love and beauty once raised the Sun up to heaven on her horns.

This god of embalming has the head of a jackal and is the most ancient of the gods. He was the overseer of mummification, and then guided the dead to the afterlife.

The town of Bubastis believed cats to be sacred. Bastet, the cat goddess, was worshiped there.

The god of learning and science holds a writing implement in his hand. He has the head of an ibis, a water bird found along the banks of the Nile.

This god is shown with the head of a crocodile, sometimes wearing the horns of Amon-Re and the solar disk. He symbolized the fertility of the Nile.

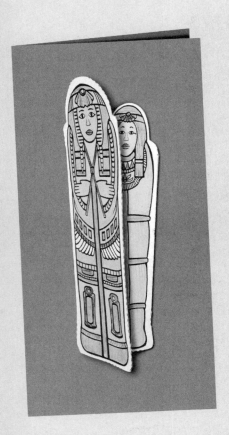

WHERE'S MY MUMMY?

The fascinating process of mummification grew out of the Egyptian belief that the body was needed in the afterlife. Students make a book that depicts how a mummy was placed in several coffins. The steps of mummification complete the book.

STEPS TO FOLLOW

1. Review with students the information about mummification on the "About Religion" page. Then read and discuss the mummification process on page 55.

2. Students fold the construction paper in half, cut out the title section, and glue it onto the front of the booklet. They glue the mummification process to the back of the booklet.

3. Direct students to cut out the mummy on page 53 and cover it with small pieces of gauze bandage. Overlap the pieces for a more authentic look.

4. Open the booklet and glue the mummy in the center of the right-hand page.

5. Color and cut out the two coffins on page 54.

6. Make creases on the fold lines and glue each tab down so the coffins go on top of the mummy, placing the smaller of the two down first.

MATERIALS

- pages 53–55, reproduced for each student
- 12" (30.5 cm) square of construction paper
- roll of gauze bandage
- crayons or colored pencils
- scissors
- glue

EMC 3706 · Ancient Egypt · ©2003 by Evan-Moor Corp.

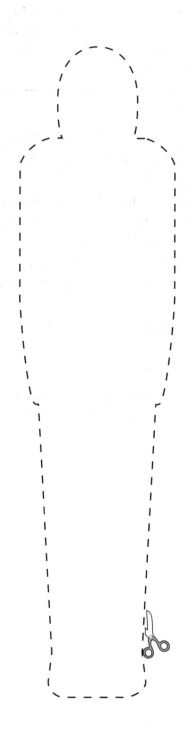

WHERE'S MY MUMMY?

NAME _____

WHERE'S MY MUMMY?

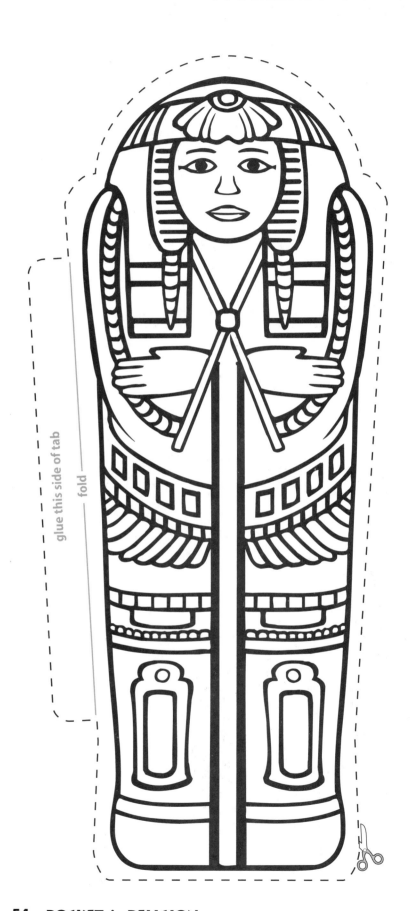

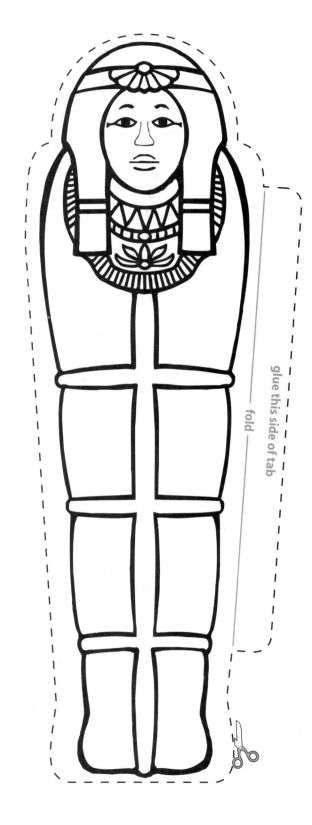

EMC 3706 · Ancient Egypt · ©2003 by Evan-Moor Corp.

👁 THE MUMMIFICATION PROCESS 👁

The 70-day mummification process began with a ceremony conducted by four priests. One of the priests dressed as the god Anubis. The inner organs were removed first. The brain was removed through the nose with a special hook and thrown away.

The liver, stomach, lungs, and intestines were removed through a cut on the left side of the body. The heart was usually left in the body. The organs were placed in special jars called canopic jars. A special type of salt called natron was added to the jars to preserve the organs.

The body was washed with oils and spices. Linen and natron were packed into the body. Then the body was covered with natron and placed on a tilted slab. The natron dried the body of its fluids, which drained onto the slab. The body was allowed to dry for at least 40 days.

The old packing was replaced and the incision sewed up. The body was rubbed with oils and resins. The nostrils were plugged with wax. Makeup was applied. The first strips of cloth were wound around the body. The process would take about 15 days.

The body was decorated with jewelry, and good-luck charms were tucked into the 20 or so layers of linen strips.

The cloth-wrapped face was covered with a mask, on which the face of the dead person was painted.

Finally, the mummy was placed in one or more coffins and was ready for the funeral procession to its final resting place. 👁

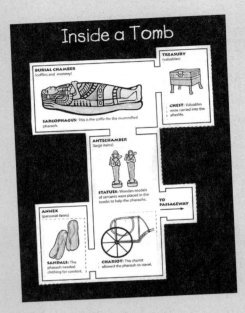

Inside a Tomb

MATERIALS

- pages 57 and 58, reproduced for students
- 9" x 12" (23 x 30.5 cm) black construction paper
- white crayon or colored pencil
- scissors
- glue

INSIDE A TOMB

When archaeologist Howard Carter's team opened the tomb of Tutankhamen in 1922, they discovered a multitude of luxuries stored for the pharaoh's use in the afterlife. Students place typical items in the correct rooms of the tomb.

STEPS TO FOLLOW

1. Read and discuss the information about treasures found in tombs of the pharaohs.

2. Students color and cut out the tomb items on page 58 and glue them in the correct area of the tomb on page 57.

3. After cutting around the outside of the tomb, students glue the tomb cutout onto the black paper.

4. Direct students to cut out and glue the information paragraph to the construction paper.

5. On the top of the page, students should write the title "Inside a Tomb," using a white crayon or a white colored pencil.

EMC 3706 · Ancient Egypt · ©2003 by Evan-Moor Corp.

INSIDE A TOMB

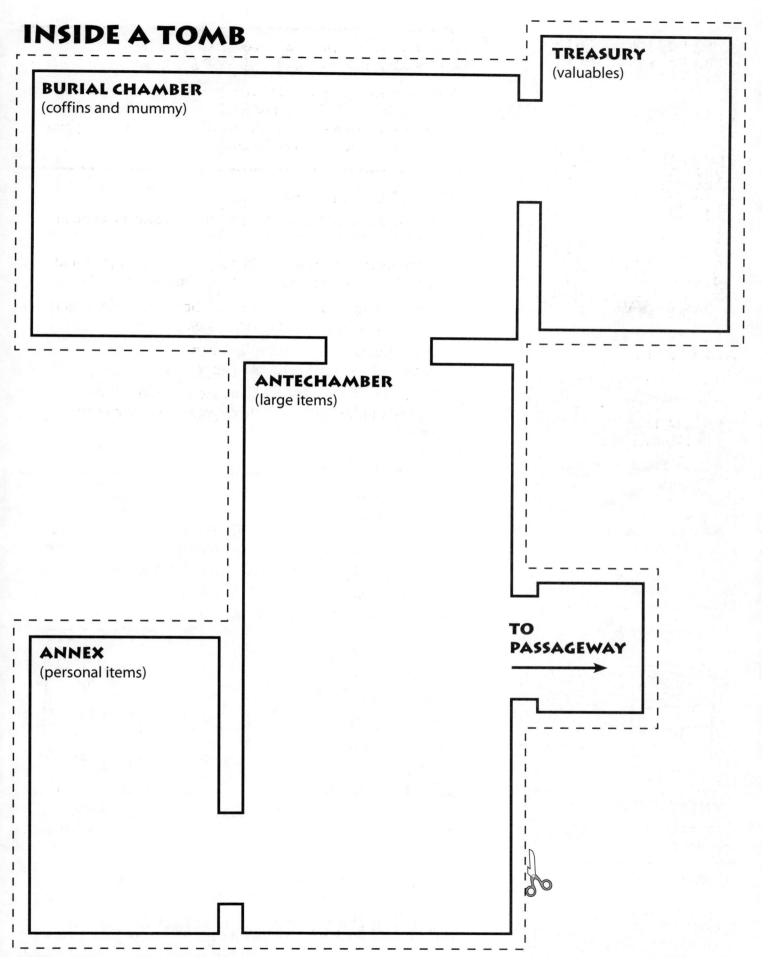

BURIAL CHAMBER
(coffins and mummy)

TREASURY
(valuables)

ANTECHAMBER
(large items)

ANNEX
(personal items)

TO PASSAGEWAY

INSIDE A TOMB

Pharaohs were buried in magnificent tombs with all the luxuries of life so that they could enjoy them in the afterlife. In 1922 British archaeologist Howard Carter and his team opened the tomb of Tutankhamen, the Boy King. Inside they discovered beds, a throne, bouquets of flowers, chariots, weapons, tools, statues of gods, boats, clothing, jewelry, and food.

SARCOPHAGUS: This is the coffin for the mummified pharaoh.

STATUES: Wooden models of servants were placed in the tombs to help the pharaohs.

CHEST: Valuables were carried into the afterlife.

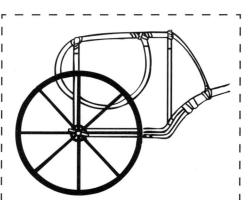

CHARIOT: The chariot allowed the pharaoh to travel.

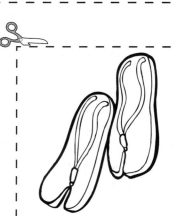

SANDALS: The pharaoh needed clothing for comfort.

EMC 3706 · Ancient Egypt ·©2003 by Evan-Moor Corp.

Pocket 5

ARCHITECTURE

FAST FACTS

Architecture . . . . **page 60**
See page 2 for information on how to prepare the Fast
Facts bookmark and pocket label. Use the bookmark
for a quick review during transition times throughout
the day.

ABOUT

Architecture . . . . **page 61**
Reproduce this page for students. Read about and
discuss the architecture of ancient Egypt, highlighting
important information to remember. Incorporate
library and multimedia resources that are available.

ART REFERENCE

Architecture . . . . **page 62**
Use this reproducible page as a reference for the
activities in the pocket.

ACTIVITIES

Pyramid Power . . . . **pages 63 & 64**
Students make a book showing a pyramid being built
from start to finish.

The Great Pyramid at Giza . . . . **pages 65–67**
Students make a pyramid-shaped book containing information about the Great Pyramid and
a cross section showing the chambers of Khufu's tomb.

Egyptian Mathematics . . . . **page 68**
Students get a chance to use hieroglyphic numerals to write statistics about the Great Pyramid.
Answer key provided on inside back cover.

An Egyptian Home . . . . **pages 69–71**
Open this folded book to view a cross section of an Egyptian home that a skilled craftsman or
government official might have lived in.

Create a Courtyard . . . . **pages 72–74**
Students create a "pop-up" courtyard such as might have been found in the home of a wealthy
Egyptian.

Summing It Up
Reproduce page 13 from Pocket 1 for each student. Students review the information learned in
this pocket, choose three pieces of information, and write a paragraph as a summary of the pocket.

ARCHITECTURE

ARCHITECTURE
FAST FACTS

- The Great Pyramid is the largest limestone building in the world. When first built, the structure stood 481 feet (147 meters) tall, as tall as a 40-story building.

- The Great Pyramid has lost 30 feet (9 meters) off the top over the years. It is now 451 feet (138 meters) tall.

- The pyramids were built primarily as tombs for pharaohs.

- Historians think that it took 20,000 workers between 10 and 20 years to build the Great Pyramid.

- Construction on a pharaoh's tomb began when he took office and continued until he died. The shorter a pharaoh's life, the smaller his temple would be.

- Egypt gave an ancient obelisk to both the U.S. and to Great Britain. You can see them in New York City's Central Park and on the bank of the Thames River in London.

- The tops of columns of some Egyptian temples were carved to look like palm trees or papyrus reeds.

ABOUT ARCHITECTURE

Egyptians made it easy for us to learn about how they lived and what they believed. How? They built buildings that lasted. Many of their ancient structures remain intact today despite centuries of wear due to sandstorms, robbers, and other destructive forces.

Homes of the common people did not weather the test of time, however. The average home was made from mud bricks that had been dried in the sun. Some homes had more than one story, the first story for a business and one or two others for living space. In addition, some had an underground cellar for storage. Homes of the nobility were larger. They often had wall decorations and tiled floors.

Perhaps the most famous Egyptian buildings are the massive stone pyramids. They were usually built as tombs for pharaohs. It took an enormous amount of human labor, stone (primarily limestone and granite), and time to construct them. Along the Nile River, the ruins of dozens of ancient pyramids (particularly the Great Pyramid at Giza, which is near Cairo) still stand today. In fact, the pyramids are the only one of the Seven Wonders of the Ancient World that still exist.

We do not know for certain how ancient Egyptians built the pyramids, although there are plenty of theories. People used to believe that the pyramids were built by thousands of slaves. However, most historians now agree that everyday Egyptians built the pyramids.

Some people claim that the construction of the pyramids required a technology that was lost to time and that we could not build them today! It is hard to believe, but very few modern cranes would be strong enough to move the blocks of heavy limestone that form the pyramids. The Egyptians did not use mortar to hold the stones together. Even without mortar, the stones supposedly fit together so perfectly that you could not insert a knife blade between two of them.

The first type of pyramid the Egyptians built was a style called ziggurat. Ziggurats were made of mud bricks. The sides of ziggurats were not straight slopes like the familiar triangular pyramids that would come later. They look like giant steps, and were therefore called step pyramids.

The Egyptians built other distinctive structures as well. One was a pylon, or large wall, decorated with carvings that stood at the entrance of temples. The other was an obelisk, or stone column, which was wider at its base and rose to a point. They were also erected at the entrances of temples. Obelisks were used as ancient "message boards"—they were inscribed with the names of rulers and religious events. They were often engraved with hieroglyphs about sun worship.

ARCHITECTURE

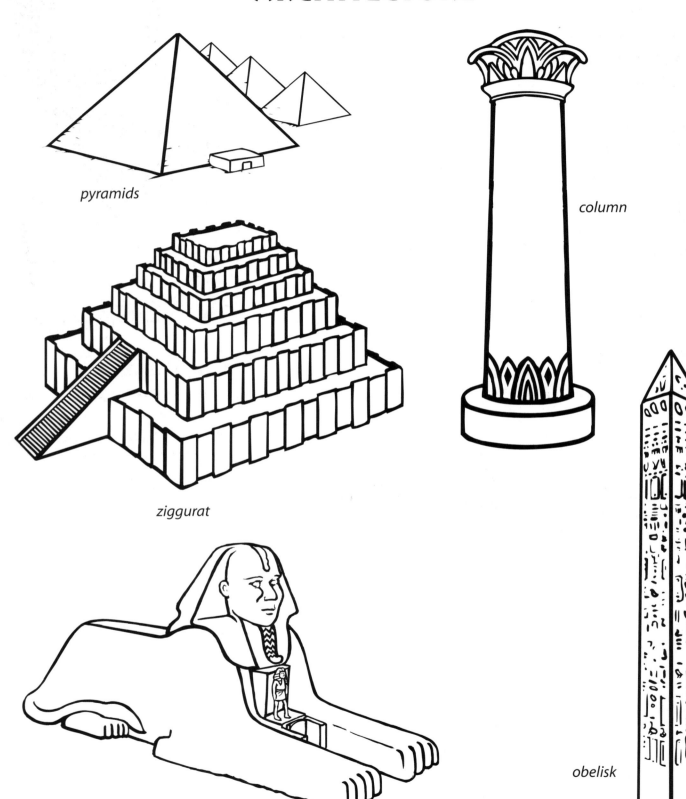

pyramids

column

ziggurat

obelisk

sphinx

    EMC 3706 · Ancient Egypt · ©2003 by Evan-Moor Corp.

PYRAMID POWER

Students put the steps for building a pyramid in order. Then they display the steps in a "poof" book.

STEPS TO FOLLOW

1. Direct students to color and cut apart the cover and the five steps.

2. Have students follow the directions to make a poof book to display the pyramid-building process.

   a. Fold the large piece of construction paper as shown.

   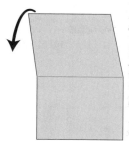 

   b. Open the paper and cut on the fold as shown, stopping at the horizontal fold.

   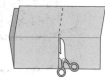

   c. Open up the paper completely. Fold the paper in half the long way with the cut side on top. Push in the ends. "Poof," you have a minibook.

   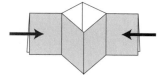

   d. Students read the steps for building a pyramid and decide on the correct order. Then students glue the cover and the steps on the pages of the book.

MATERIALS

- page 64, reproduced for each student
- 12" x 18" (30.5 x 45.5 cm) construction paper
- crayons or marking pens
- scissors
- glue

PYRAMID POWER

Workers then made a huge ramp and dragged the stone blocks up on rollers.

It took thousands of workers many years to complete just one straight-sided pyramid. The first step included leveling the site where the pyramid was to be placed.

PYRAMID POWER

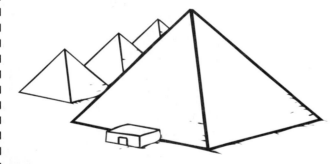

NAME _____

Ropes and levers were used to place the huge blocks in the correct position.

Stonemasons cut limestone into blocks. It is said that each block of stone weighed from 2 to 14 tons.

Casing stones were used to fill in the steps. Level by level, from the top to the bottom, the stones were fitted and chiseled to a flat surface. Then they were polished brightly to make the pyramid shine.

EMC 3706 · Ancient Egypt ·©2003 by Evan-Moor Corp.

THE GREAT PYRAMID AT GIZA

Take a look inside the Great Pyramid at Giza. Students make a pyramid shape book to display facts about Khufu's monumental tomb.

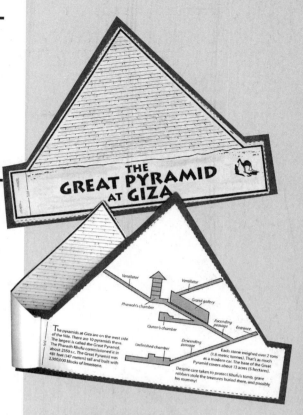

STEPS TO FOLLOW

1. Read and discuss the information about the Great Pyramid on page 67. Point out aspects of the tomb as shown in the cross section. Bring in additional information and pictures to enrich the discussion.

2. Direct students to cut out the pyramid shapes on pages 66 and 67.

3. Students glue page 67 (pyramid cross section) to the brown construction paper.

4. Next, students cut the backing, leaving a brown border around the pyramid shape.

5. Finally, students attach the cover (the outside of the pyramid) by stapling on the left side only.

MATERIALS

- pages 66 and 67, reproduced for each student
- 9" x 12" (23 x 30.5 cm) brown construction paper
- scissors
- glue
- stapler

THE GREAT PYRAMID AT GIZA

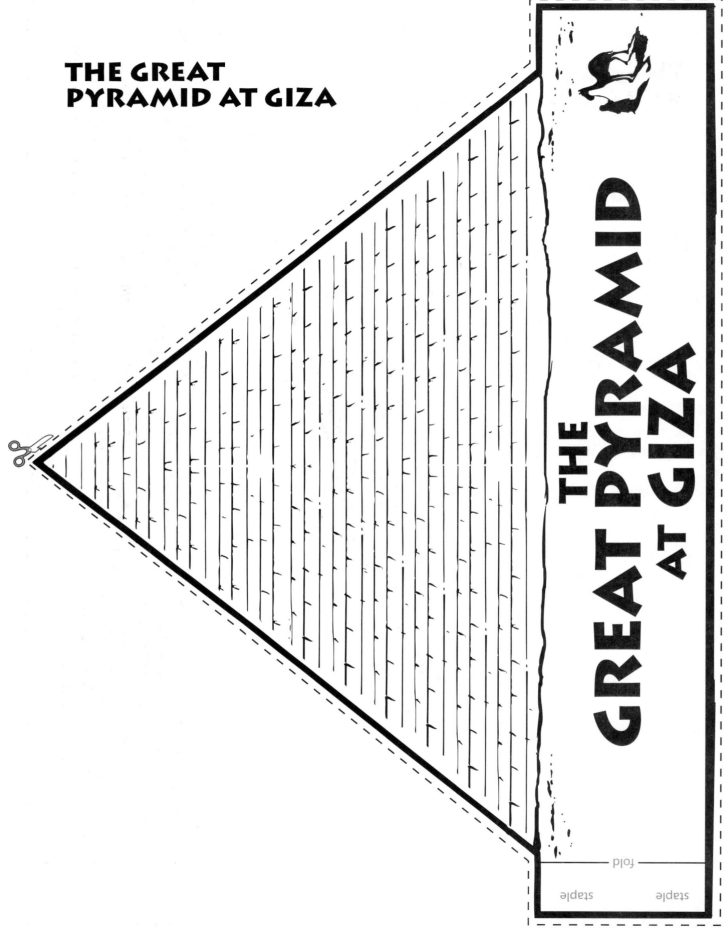

THE GREAT PYRAMID AT GIZA

fold

staple   staple

EMC 3706 · Ancient Egypt ·©2003 by Evan-Moor Corp.

THE GREAT PYRAMID AT GIZA

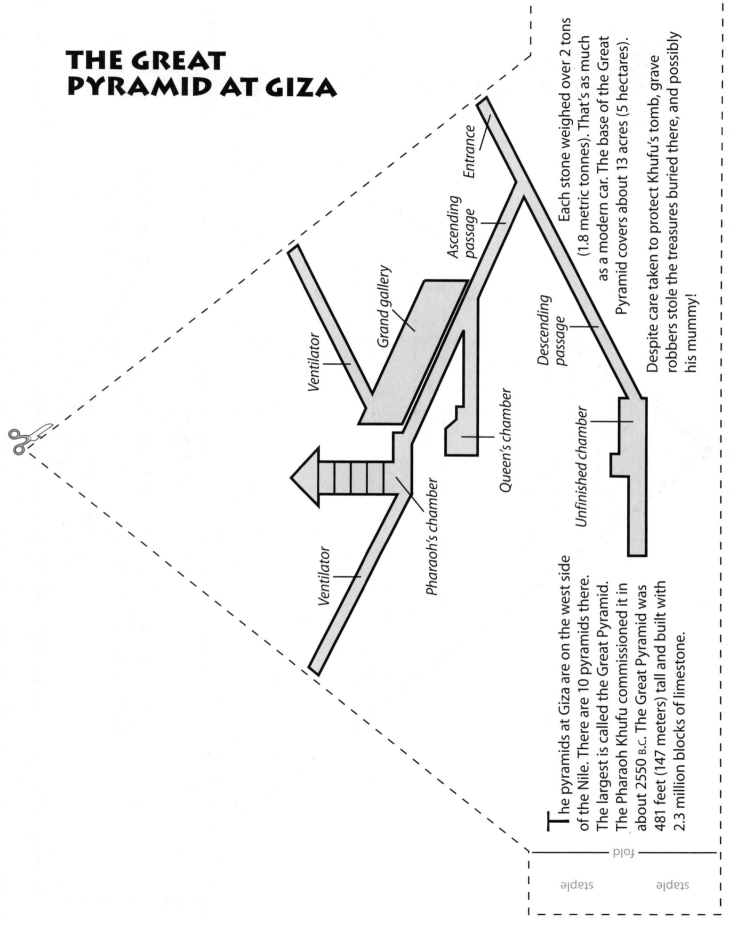

Entrance

Ascending passage

Grand gallery

Ventilator

Ventilator

Pharaoh's chamber

Queen's chamber

Descending passage

Unfinished chamber

Each stone weighed over 2 tons (1.8 metric tonnes). That's as much as a modern car. The base of the Great Pyramid covers about 13 acres (5 hectares).

Despite care taken to protect Khufu's tomb, grave robbers stole the treasures buried there, and possibly his mummy!

The pyramids at Giza are on the west side of the Nile. There are 10 pyramids there. The largest is called the Great Pyramid. The Pharaoh Khufu commissioned it in about 2550 B.C. The Great Pyramid was 481 feet (147 meters) tall and built with 2.3 million blocks of limestone.

fold

staple

staple

Name: _____

EGYPTIAN MATHEMATICS

Egyptians used hieroglyphic numerals throughout their long history. This was a base 10 system of hieroglyphs for numerals. This meant that they had separate symbols for one unit, one ten, one hundred, one thousand, one ten thousand, one hundred thousand, and one million.

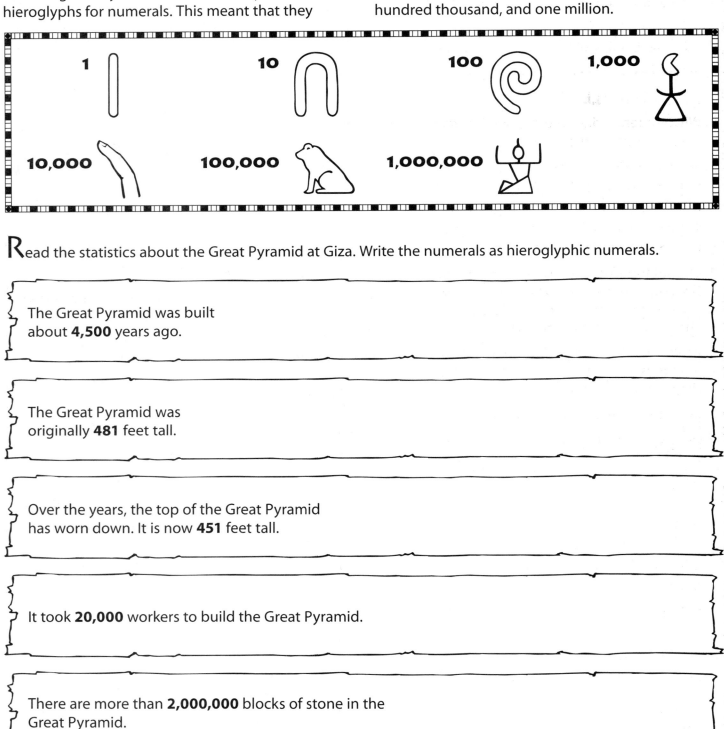

Read the statistics about the Great Pyramid at Giza. Write the numerals as hieroglyphic numerals.

The Great Pyramid was built about **4,500** years ago.

The Great Pyramid was originally **481** feet tall.

Over the years, the top of the Great Pyramid has worn down. It is now **451** feet tall.

It took **20,000** workers to build the Great Pyramid.

There are more than **2,000,000** blocks of stone in the Great Pyramid.

    EMC 3706 · Ancient Egypt ·©2003 by Evan-Moor Corp.

AN EGYPTIAN HOME

The homes of middle-class working families were all very similar to each other. Houses were joined in rows on both sides of the street. Sometimes houses were two or three stories tall.

Students make a folded book that shows a cross section of a typical middle-class house and label the descriptions of each room.

STEPS TO FOLLOW

1. With students, view and discuss the cross section of the Egyptian home on page 70.

2. Instruct students to measure 4½" (11.5 cm) from the top of the construction paper and fold the paper down. Make a similar fold up from the bottom.

3. Color the home diagram. Cut it out and glue it to the inside center section of the construction paper.

4. Cut out the seven boxes that describe parts of the home. Glue the boxes in the top and bottom sections of the construction paper, above and below the home diagram. There is no correct order to do this.

5. Read each description. Decide which part of the home it describes. Write the number found on the diagram in the circle on the description box.

6. Close the folder. Glue the title on the top flap.

7. Decorate the folder with stamped papyrus flowers.

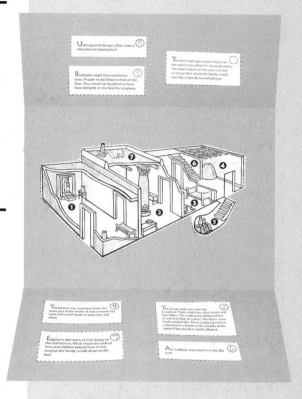

MATERIALS

- pages 70 and 71, reproduced for each student
- 12" x 18" (30.5 x 45.5 cm) yellow or light blue construction paper
- ruler
- crayons or colored pencils
- scissors
- glue
- papyrus stamp from page 10
- green tempera paint

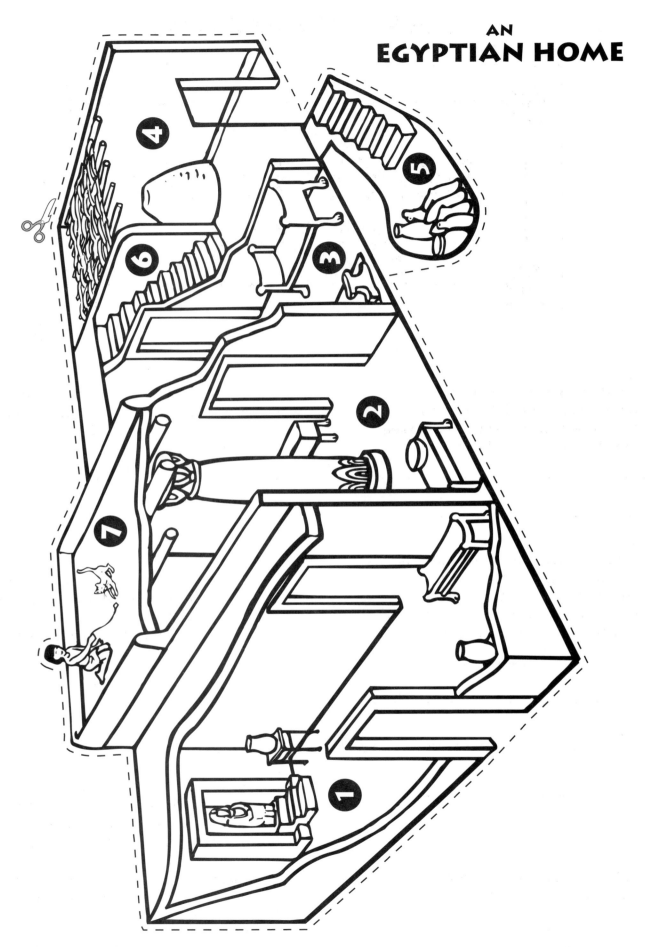

EMC 3706 · Ancient Egypt ·©2003 by Evan-Moor Corp.

AN
EGYPTIAN HOME

Bedrooms might have one bed or none. People would sleep on mats on the floor. They would use headrests to keep from being bit on the head by scorpions.

The kitchen was separated from the main part of the house. It had a round clay oven and a roof made of branches and straw.

The first room you would enter from the street was called the reception room. The main feature of this room was the recessed altar where the family would worship a friendly household god.

Egyptians did much of their living on the roof terrace. Meals might be cooked here and children played here. In hot weather the family would sleep on the roof.

An outdoor stairway led to the flat roof.

Underground storage cellars were a cool place for storing food.

The living room was sparsely furnished. There might be a few stools and low tables. The walls were whitewashed or painted blue or yellow. The floors were hard-packed dirt. There might have been a decorative column in the middle of the room if the dwellers could afford it.

CREATE A COURTYARD

Wealthy Egyptians had large homes with lovely courtyards with pools, fountains, and statuary. Students create a pop-up showing how such a garden courtyard might have looked.

MATERIALS

- pages 73 and 74, reproduced for each student
- 9" x 12" (23 x 30.5 cm) construction paper
- crayons, marking pens, or colored pencils
- scissors
- glue

STEPS TO FOLLOW

1. Instruct students to color the items on pages 73 and 74.

2. Students then cut and fold the pop-up form as shown.

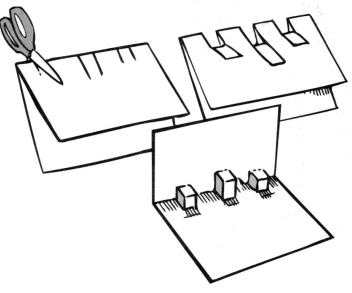

3. Have students fold the construction paper in half and glue the pop-up form in the construction paper folder.

Pop-up tab

4. Students finish the pop-up by cutting out the columns and the statue and gluing them to the front of the pop-up tabs.

5. Direct students to glue the title and information box to the front of the folder.

EMC 3706 • Ancient Egypt •©2003 by Evan-Moor Corp.

CREATE A COURTYARD

fold

fold

fold

fold

fold

column here

statue here

column here

fold

fold

fold

CREATE A COURTYARD

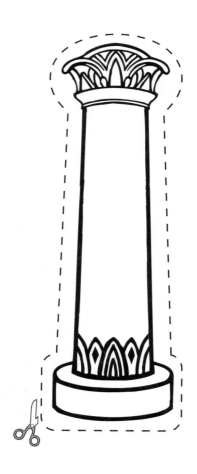  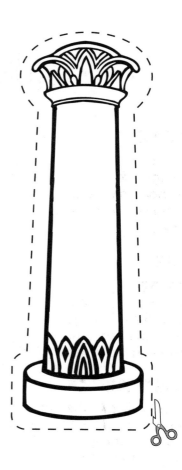

AN EGYPTIAN COURTYARD

If you were a wealthy Egyptian from the pharaoh's court, you would have a spacious home with many rooms and a large garden or courtyard. The courtyard would be very peaceful. A large wall kept out the noise. You could walk on paths passing by pools, fountains, and fine columns and statues. Pharaohs often placed statues of themselves in the courtyards of their palaces.

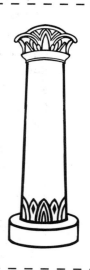

          EMC 3706 · Ancient Egypt ·©2003 by Evan-Moor Corp.

LANGUAGE

FAST FACTS

Language. . . . . **page 76**

See page 2 for information on how to prepare the Fast Facts bookmark and pocket label. Use the bookmark for a quick review during transition times throughout the day.

ABOUT

Language. . . . . **page 77**

Reproduce this page for students. Read about and discuss the language of ancient Egypt, highlighting important information to remember. Incorporate library and multimedia resources that are available.

ART REFERENCE

Hieroglyphic Alphabet . . . . **page 78**

Use this reproducible page as a reference for the activities in the pocket. (Note: Hieroglyphic symbols changed throughout ancient Egyptian history. Reference sources may vary in their depiction of some symbols.)

ACTIVITIES

Your Own Cartouche . . . . **page 79**

Students make cartouche name tags in hieroglyphs.

A Reverse Dictionary. . . . . **page 80**

Students become word detectives by translating the definitions on a representation of a page from an ancient Egyptian dictionary. Reproduce page 78 for students to use as reference. Answer key provided on inside back cover.

Scribes and Papyrus—Egyptian Essentials . . . . **page 81**

All recordkeeping in Egypt depended on the scribes. And the scribes depended on scrolls of papyrus to write on. Students learn about both of these essentials. (Note: Papyrus is found eight times in the word search.) Answer key provided on inside back cover.

Summing It Up

Reproduce page 13 from Pocket 1 for each student. Students review the information learned in this pocket, choose three pieces of information, and write a paragraph as a summary of the pocket.

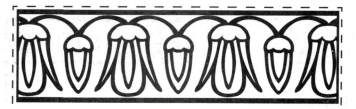

LANGUAGE

LANGUAGE

FAST FACTS

- The word *hieroglyph* is from the Greek, meaning "sacred carving."

- Egyptians may have learned about writing from the Sumerians.

- The Egyptians were the first to use papyrus writing paper.

- Hieroglyphs could be read from left to right, right to left, or vertically depending on the way the signs faced.

- Demotic writing came into use late in ancient Egypt's history. The word *demotic* means "the people's writing."

- Egyptians believed hieroglyphics were magical and that writing was a sacred act.

- The Egyptian spoken language was related to the languages of southwestern Asia and to some in northern Africa. It was eventually replaced with Arabic.

ABOUT LANGUAGE

Hieroglyphics was the original writing system of ancient Egypt. It was an alphabet that consisted of hieroglyphs, or picture symbols. They may look easy to understand, but there were many ways to use them. In earlier times, a hieroglyph was a literal symbol for an object. For example, a picture of a bird would mean "bird." Eventually, a hieroglyph could also be used as a sound or syllable—the way we now use a letter or a combination of letters from our alphabet. A picture of a bird might be a syllable in a word that had nothing to do with birds. Some hieroglyphs represented more than one letter. For example, a horned snake (sometimes called a viper) was both the letter *F* and the letter *V.* Some letters could be represented by more than one hieroglyph (*H* was sometimes a shelter and other times what looks like a twisted rope). At first, there were about 700 hieroglyphic symbols, but that number grew over time. Vowels and punctuation were not represented in hieroglyphics.

Most Egyptians were not literate. That is, they could not read or write. During some of ancient Egypt's history, only government officials called scribes were literate.

As you can imagine, it must have been hard to write quickly with hieroglyphs. That is why Egyptians developed two other writing systems that were easier to scribble down in a hurry. They were called hieratic writing and demotic writing. The hieroglyphic system was used mainly for tombs or temples, while the other languages were used for keeping records. However, hieroglyphs have also been found carved into stone and pottery and written with black ink on scrolls of papyrus.

Egyptians began using hieroglyphs soon after the First Dynasty began, around 3100 B.C. The last hieroglyphic inscription historians have found is dated 394 A.D. Soon after that, hieroglyphics became a "dead" language, meaning no one used it anymore. It wasn't until the early 1800s that the modern world learned how to translate hieroglyphics, thanks to an amazing archeological find called the Rosetta Stone.

In 1799 a broken piece of stone that was only 3' 9" (114 cm) long and 2' 4½" (72 cm) wide unlocked a great mystery. A French soldier accidentally uncovered the unusual slab of stone outside Rosetta, a city near Alexandria in Egypt. The stone dated back to 196 B.C. Text had been carved into it in three languages: hieroglyphic (pictures and symbols), demotic (everyday language of the people), and Greek. Egyptologists at the time knew how to read both Greek and demotic, so they could tell that the text was identical in both languages. They deduced that the text must also be the same in hieroglyphic, and studied the Rosetta Stone to figure out how to read hieroglyphics.

HIEROGLYPHIC ALPHABET

A eagle	**B** leg	**C** **as in *cat*** basket **as in *cent*** folded cloth	**D** hand
E two reed flowers	**F** horned viper	**G** a stand for a jar	**H** reed shelter
I reed flower	**J** snake	**K** basket	**L** lion
M owl	**N** water	**O** chick	**P** stool
Q hill	**R** mole	**S** folded cloth	**T** loaf of bread
U chick	**V** horned viper	**W** chick	**X** **sounds like *k + s*** **as in *six***
Y two reed flowers	**Z** a bolt	**CH** tethering rope	**SH** pond

EMC 3706 · Ancient Egypt · ©2003 by Evan-Moor Corp.

YOUR OWN CARTOUCHE

Students create name tags with their names spelled in hieroglyphs. Students may wear their name tags before storing them in the pocket.

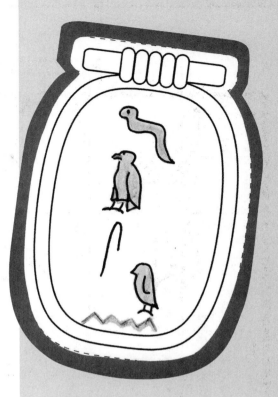

STEPS TO FOLLOW

1. With students, study the hieroglyphs on page 78. Point out that hieroglyphs stood for sounds, not letters. However, for the exercises in the pocket, students will use the symbols as letters.

2. Students use a pencil to sketch out their first name in hieroglyphs on the cartouche pattern. Students then color the hieroglyphs.

3. Have students glue the cartouche to black construction paper and cut out the cartouche, leaving a border.

4. Students apply a piece of looped clear tape to the back and stick the name tag on their shirts.

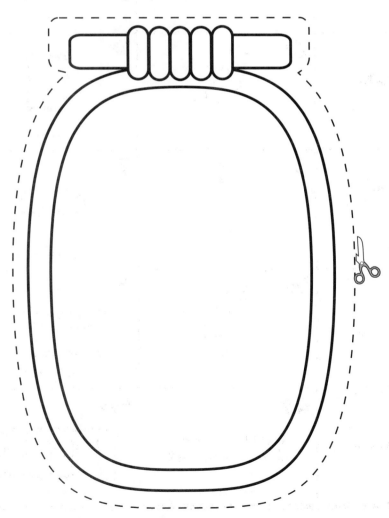

MATERIALS

- cartouche pattern (left), reproduced for each student
- hieroglyphic alphabet on page 78, reproduced for each student
- 4" x 6" (10 x 15 cm) black construction paper
- pencil
- crayons or marking pens
- scissors
- glue
- clear tape

Name: _____

A REVERSE DICTIONARY

You've just found a page written in hieroglyphics from an ancient Egyptian dictionary. The papyrus has somehow survived over thousands of years, but some of the ink has not. The definitions are still there, but the words that are being defined have worn away. It's up to you to help!

1 Translate each hieroglyphic definition into English, using the hieroglyphic alphabet on page 78. The first one has been done for you.

2 Determine what word is being defined and write it on the line (in English). You are given a hint for each: the number of letters in the word.

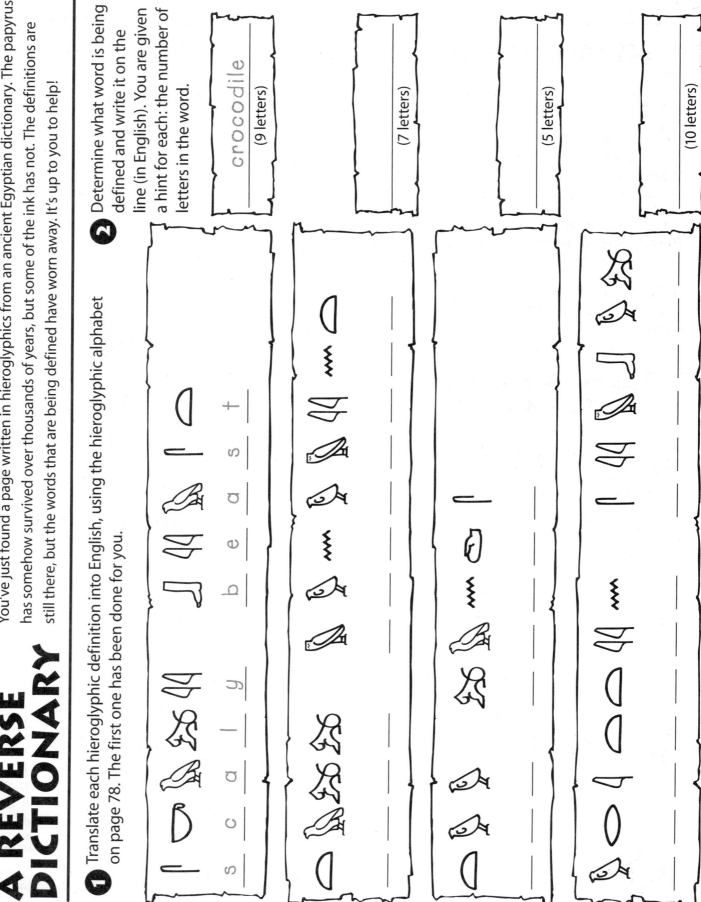

s c a l y b e a s t

crocodile
(9 letters)

(7 letters)

(5 letters)

(10 letters)

EMC 3706 · Ancient Egypt ·©2003 by Evan-Moor Corp.

Name: _____

SCRIBES AND PAPYRUS—EGYPTIAN ESSENTIALS

THE ALL-IMPORTANT SCRIBE

Most Egyptians could not read or write. Even pharaohs depended on scribes to write for them. Scribes had to write everything from legal documents to love letters for people.

It took seven years of school to become a scribe. The teachers were very strict. Boys who did not work hard might be beaten.

Scribes wrote on scrolls of papyrus. A thin, sharpened reed dipped in ink was used to write on papyrus.

HELP THE SCRIBE DECIPHER THIS MESSAGE.

_____

_____

_____

HOW TO MAKE PAPYRUS

- A papyrus plant can grow 13 feet (4 meters) tall.

- The soft pith inside the stems was sliced into very thin strips.

- The strips were laid side by side. More strips going the opposite direction were laid on top.

- A cloth was placed over the layers, and the papyrus was beaten with a mallet to squash the strips together.

- The dry paper was smoothed and polished with a stone.

- Sheets of papyrus were joined together to make a roll.

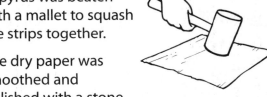

How many times can you find the word **papyrus** in this puzzle? Circle and count.

```
P P A P Y R U S P A P
A A P A P Y R U S A A
P Y P P R P A R P R P
S U R Y P A P Y U A Y
Y R U R R Y R P S Y R
P A P U R U S A U P U
R S Y S S A S P R P S
```

NUMBER FOUND: _____

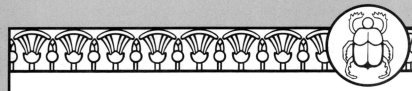

ARTS AND RECREATION

FAST FACTS

Arts and Recreation . . . . **page 83**
See page 2 for information on how to prepare the Fast Facts bookmark and pocket label. Use the bookmark for a quick review during transition times throughout the day.

ABOUT

Arts and Recreation . . . . **page 84**
Reproduce this page for students. Read about and discuss the arts and recreation of ancient Egypt, highlighting important information to remember. Incorporate library and multimedia resources that are available.

ART REFERENCE

Frontalism . . . . **page 85**
Use this reproducible page as a reference for the activities in the pocket.

ACTIVITIES

Face Front . . . . **page 86**
Students need to follow directions precisely to be able to draw Egyptian figures using the style called frontalism.

The Great Sphinx . . . . **pages 87–89**
The Sphinx at Giza is one of the best-known landmarks in the world. Students make a shape book and write facts about the Sphinx.

Sacred Felines . . . . **pages 90 & 91**
Students write a poem inside a cat "statue" to show respect for ancient Egypt's unofficial mascot.

Let's Play Senet . . . . **pages 92 & 93**
Nobility and commoners alike played this board game. Many senet boards have been found in tombs. Students will enjoy playing this ancient game that is similar to backgammon.

Trivia Along the Nile . . . . **page 94**
Students review the information in their pockets, write four trivia questions, and then quiz each other.

Summing It Up
Reproduce page 13 from Pocket 1 for each student. Students review the information learned in this pocket, choose three pieces of information, and write a paragraph as a summary of the pocket.

    EMC 3706 · Ancient Egypt ·©2003 by Evan-Moor Corp.

ARTS AND RECREATION

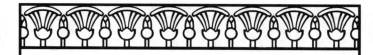

ARTS AND RECREATION

FAST FACTS

- Most of the art pieces that have survived were carved in stone.

- Paint was made from minerals. Paintbrushes were wooden sticks with frayed ends.

- The word *sphinx* is a Greek word that means "to bind." In a Greek myth, the sphinx strangled its victims.

- The face and body of the Sphinx at Giza were painted red in ancient Egypt. It once had a beard that has since crumbled off. The Sphinx was buried in the sand for centuries.

- A sistrum, an instrument similar to a rattle, was used in religious worship.

- Both males and females sang at rituals and parties in ancient Egypt.

- Originally, Egyptian men hunted foxes and hyenas in the desert on foot. Later they used horses and chariots.

- A board game called senet (similar to backgammon) was popular with both adults and children.

ABOUT
ARTS AND RECREATION

Painting, sculpture, music, literature, and sports were all a part of ancient Egyptian society. The arts commonly appeared in religious buildings and ceremonies to honor gods, goddesses, and pharaohs. Some tomb walls were painted with real historical events, such as military victories, while others were fictional. These scenes were more than decorations. Egyptians believed that in the afterlife, the scenes would become real places where they would spend time.

Hieroglyphics was the ancient Egyptian system of picture-writing, but it was art as well. Gods, goddesses, and pharaohs were drawn in the familiar ancient Egyptian style: their faces are in profile (from the side), but their torsos are facing front. This style is called frontalism. Although many people observe that the figures look stiff and almost like cartoons, frontalism was actually a symbol of respect. Slaves and animals were often drawn more realistically.

Sphinxes were large stone statues carved to protect important buildings. They represented the greatness of pharaohs and usually had the body of a lion and the head of a human, hawk, or ram. Some had wings and a serpent tail. The most well-known is the Sphinx near the Great Pyramid at Giza. Historians believe it was built around 2500 B.C., most likely in honor of Khafre, a pharaoh in the Fourth Dynasty. It is 240 feet (73 m) long and 65 feet (20 m) tall. That's a big security guard!

Smaller sculptures and crafts such as pottery were made from wood, ivory, gold, bronze, and glass. These were often sculptures of deities, rulers, and animals. Cat figurines were very popular because Egyptians considered cats both sacred and useful—they protected grain supplies from mice.

Subjects of literature included mathematics, astronomy, medicine, magic, stories, and instructions on how to live a good life.

Music was a part of religious functions, joyous festivals, and parties thrown by the nobility. Musicians played harps and lutes. They also had wind instruments such as flutes, and percussion instruments such as drums. Singers often performed with the music.

The Nile River was the most significant source of recreation. People fished, went sailing, swam, and played games there. Men (particularly from the nobility) liked to hunt crocodiles and hippopotamuses there, and other animals in the nearby desert. People also participated in sports, such as boxing, hockey, and gymnastics.

FRONTALISM

Only one eye is shown. It looks as it would from the front. Eyes were outlined in black.

The shoulders and chest (torso) are drawn as seen from the front. Arms may show action to explain what the figure is doing.

The lower body (hips, legs, and feet) are drawn from the side.

The head and neck are drawn from the side (profile).

FACE FRONT

This activity gives students a chance to draw figures in the Egyptian frontalism style. In frontalism the head and neck of the figure is drawn in profile; the shoulders and chest are drawn as seen from the front; and the hips, legs, and feet are drawn in profile.

STEPS TO FOLLOW

1. As a class, study the figures on page 85 and discuss the major aspects of frontalism. If possible, provide other examples from reference materials.

2. Students use the model of frontalism on page 85 to draw one or two figures on the tan paper. They should first sketch lightly with pencil and then color with marking pens or colored pencils. Encourage students to add their own touches by changing the poses; adding jewelry, wigs, and clothing as they wish; or putting the arms in various positions.

3. Students tear around the edge of the paper to give a rough papyrus appearance.

4. Direct students to glue the tan paper onto the black construction paper, leaving a border around the edge.

MATERIALS

- page 85, reproduced for each student
- 10" x 7" (25.5 x 18 cm) tan or manila paper
- 9" x 12" (23 x 30.5 cm) black construction paper
- pencil
- marking pens or colored pencils
- glue

   EMC 3706 · Ancient Egypt ·©2003 by Evan-Moor Corp.

THE GREAT SPHINX

Students make a sphinx shape book and write about the well-known Sphinx at Giza.

The Sphinx near the Great Pyramid at Giza is the most well-known Sphinx. The great Sphinx was probably built around 2500 B.C. It may have been built to honor the pharaoh Khafre. The great Sphinx was 240 feet long and 65 feet wide. The Sphinx was supposed to guard the pharaoh's tomb.

THE GREAT SPHINX

STEPS TO FOLLOW

1. Refer students to the "About Arts and Recreation" information on page 84 and the bookmark on page 83. Locate the information about sphinxes and review the facts together.

2. Tell students that they are to summarize the information and write their own paragraphs about the Sphinx at Giza on the lines provided, and then cut out the sphinx shape. Depending on the capabilities of your students, you may wish to have them work in small groups or provide a topic sentence for them.

3. Remind students that the Sphinx at Giza was painted red at one time. Direct them to place the sphinx pattern on a rough surface such as a stucco or plaster wall. Using the side of the red crayon, color the sphinx.

4. Cut out the colored sphinx and staple the pattern page and the writing form together at the top.

MATERIALS

- pages 88 and 89, reproduced for each student
- pictures of the Sphinx at Giza, if possible
- red crayon
- pencil
- scissors
- stapler

Your students might enjoy trying to solve the riddle that the sphinx asked of Oedipus in Sophocles' play *Oedipus Rex*.

"What walks on four legs in the morning, two legs in the afternoon, and three legs in the evening, and whose speed is least when on the most legs?"

The answer: Humans, who crawl in the "morning" of life, walk on two legs as adults in the "afternoon" of life, and use a cane in the "evening" of life.

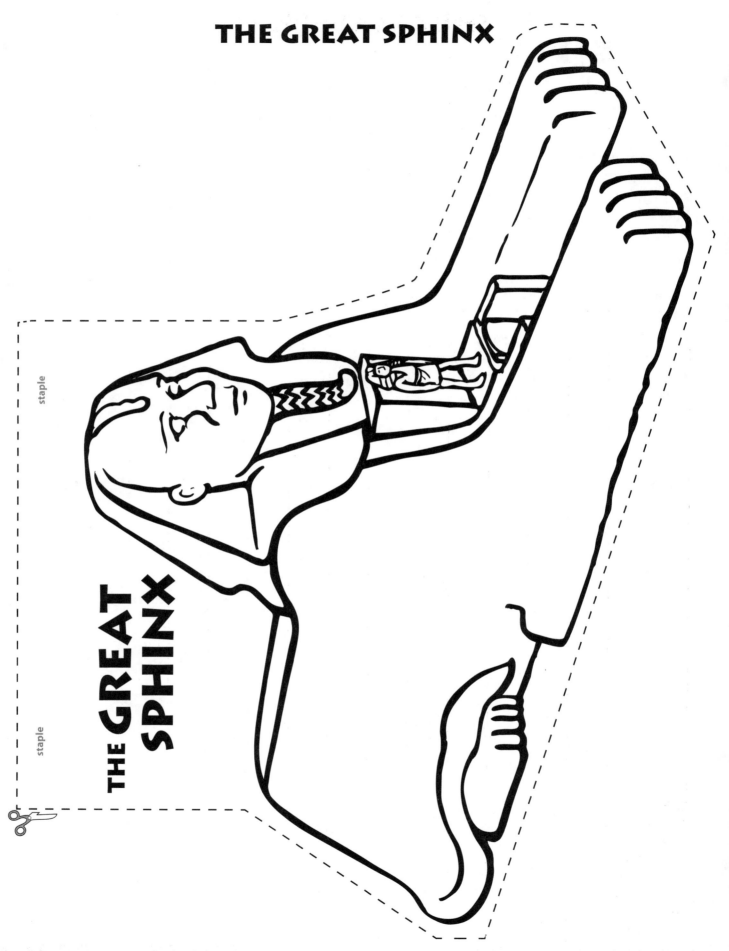

THE GREAT SPHINX

staple

staple

EMC 3706 · Ancient Egypt · ©2003 by Evan-Moor Corp.

THE GREAT SPHINX

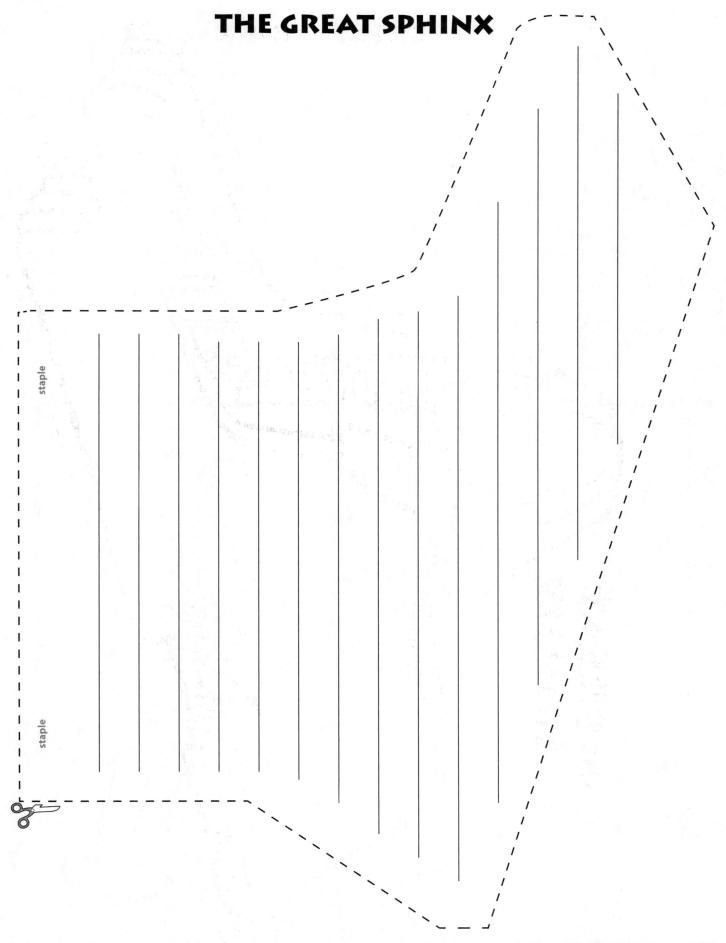

staple

staple

SACRED FELINES

Students write a poem that ancient Egyptians might have recited to show how beloved cats were and enclose the poem in a cat "statue."

STEPS TO FOLLOW

1. With students, read the information on page 91 about the importance of cats to the ancient Egyptians.

2. Students color the front of the cat pattern, cut it out, and fold to make a booklet.

3. On the inside of the booklet, students write a poem dedicated to cats in ancient Egypt. Depending on the poetry writing experience of your class, assign a type of poetry or choice of types to write. Students may write couplets, haiku, cinquains, acrostics, or other poetry forms. Examples are given below.

4. Students share their cat poems with the class.

MATERIALS

- page 91, reproduced for each student
- pencil
- scissors
- ruler

COUPLET
Oh, cat, so quiet on padded feet
We are helped when you catch mice to eat.

HAIKU
Dear goddess Bastet
Protect our family now
As we honor you.

CINQUAIN
Cat
So sleek
Hunting you go
Seeking a tasty meal
Predator

ACROSTIC
Crouching
Attacker
Triumphant

EMC 3706 · Ancient Egypt · ©2003 by Evan-Moor Corp.

SACRED FELINES

Cats were very important to ancient Egyptians. Originally, wild cats were used to rid households of snakes, rats, and mice. Then Egyptians domesticated them, and cats became pets. Many children, especially their daughters, were named after cats. Cats were seen to have mysterious and magical qualities. An Egyptian myth tells of a battle won by releasing thousands of cats onto the enemy. There were cat goddesses. The most famous one was Bastet. She was a household goddess protecting women, children, and cats. She was also the goddess of the sunrise, music, dance, pleasure, family, and birth. Cat jewelry and statues were common. Cats were even mummified and buried with their owners. At one point in Egyptian history, the penalty for killing a cat was death.

fold

fold

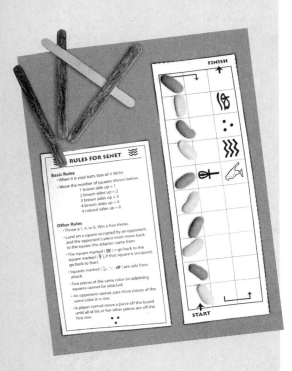

MATERIALS

- page 93, reproduced for students
- 9" x 12" (23 x 30.5 cm) construction paper
- 4 craft sticks
- brown marking pen
- 5 white beans
- 5 black beans
- reclosable bag
- paper clip

LET'S PLAY SENET

Senet was a popular Egyptian game for two players. Students make a senet board and follow the playing rules.

STEPS TO FOLLOW TO MAKE THE GAME

1. Students cut out and glue the game board and rules to the construction paper.

2. Students color one side of the craft sticks brown.

3. Store game materials in the plastic bag and paper clip to the board.

PLAYING THE GAME

1. Divide students into pairs.

2. Explain that the object of the game is to move all of your pieces around the board and off before your opponent does the same.

3. Show students how to set up the board for play. Starting with a white bean in the first square, alternate white and black beans to fill the first row as shown below.

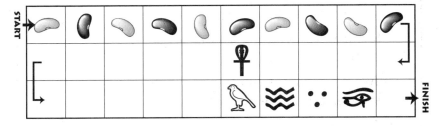

4. Explain how to start the game. Players take turns tossing all 4 sticks. The first player to get 3 brown and 1 natural faceup starts. This player will move the black beans. The other player will move the white beans. The first move by each player must be to move the last piece of his or her color.

5. Read and discuss the game rules glued to the game board. Allow time for students to ask questions before play begins.

EMC 3706 · Ancient Egypt · ©2003 by Evan-Moor Corp.

LET'S PLAY SENET

≋ RULES FOR SENET ≋

Basic Rules

- When it is your turn, toss all 4 sticks.

- Move the number of squares shown below.
  - 1 brown side up = 1
  - 2 brown sides up = 2
  - 3 brown sides up = 3
  - 4 brown sides up = 4
  - 4 natural sides up = 6

Other Rules

- Throw a 1, 4, or 6 and win a free throw.

- Land on a square occupied by an opponent, and the opponent's piece must move back to the square the attacker came from.

- The square marked (≋) = go back to the square marked (♀); if that square is occupied, go back to Start.

- Squares marked (𓅃 , ∴ , 𓂀) are safe from attack.

- Two pieces of the same color on adjoining squares cannot be attacked.

- An opponent cannot pass three pieces of the same color in a row.

- A player cannot move a piece off the board until all of his or her other pieces are off the first row.

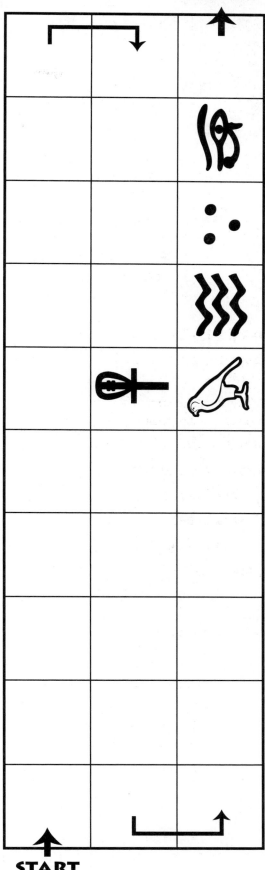

START

FINISH

TRIVIA ALONG THE NILE

Students create four trivia cards about life along the Nile and quiz each other.

MATERIALS

- four 3" x 5" (7.5 x 13 cm) index cards
- pencil
- metal ring
- hole punch
- Optional: crayons or marking pens

1. Encourage students to reread their pockets. They choose four facts they learned that they would like to use as the basis for their trivia questions.

2. Students write four questions, one per index card. They may choose from three types of questions: multiple choice, fill in the blank, or open-ended. For multiple choice, they include three choices, numbered 1, 2, and 3. Students write the answers to each of their questions on the backs of the four index cards.

3. Students pair up and quiz one another with their cards.

4. Have students punch a hole each in card and use a metal ring to fasten them together.

5. Optional:

- Once all questions are asked, take a survey about the subjects used. Make a tally list on the board to see what subjects seemed to interest students the most.

- To ensure more complete coverage of topics, you might assign a specific pocket to each small group of two to four students, so that all topics will be addressed.

- Make copies of all questions and create a class trivia game, complete with board.

    EMC 3706 · Ancient Egypt · ©2003 by Evan-Moor Corp.

ANCIENT EGYPT—REFLECTION SHEET

Name: _____ Date: _____

Directions: Please fill out this sheet after you have completed the Ancient Egypt pockets. Place your reflection sheet in the first pocket.

1. When I look through my Ancient Egypt book, I feel _____

   because _____

   _____

2. The project I liked doing the most was the _____

   because _____

   _____

3. The project I liked doing the least was the _____

   because _____

   _____

4. Three things I am most proud of in my Ancient Egypt book are _____

   _____

   _____

   _____

5. Three things I would do differently to improve my Ancient Egypt book are _____

   _____

   _____

   _____

6. Three facts that I learned about ancient Egypt that I did not know before doing this project are

   _____

   _____

   _____

7. Name three achievements or inventions of the ancient Egyptians. How has each of these
   achievements or inventions affected our lives today?

   _____

   _____

   _____

ANCIENT EGYPT—EVALUATION SHEET

Directions: Look through all the pockets and evaluate how well the activities were completed. Use the following point system:

6 outstanding	5 excellent	4 very good	3 satisfactory	2 some effort	1 little effort	0 no effort

Self-Evaluation	Peer Evaluation	Teacher Evaluation

Self-Evaluation

Name: _____

____ completed assignments

____ followed directions

____ had correct information

____ edited writing

____ showed creativity

____ displayed neatness

____ added color

____ **total points**

Comments: _____

_____
_____
_____
_____
_____
_____
_____
_____
_____
_____
_____

Peer Evaluation

Name: _____

____ completed assignments

____ followed directions

____ had correct information

____ edited writing

____ showed creativity

____ displayed neatness

____ added color

____ **total points**

Comments: _____

_____
_____
_____
_____
_____
_____
_____
_____
_____
_____
_____

Teacher Evaluation

____ completed assignments

____ followed directions

____ had correct information

____ edited writing

____ showed creativity

____ displayed neatness

____ added color

____ **total points**

____ **grade**

Comments: _____

_____
_____
_____
_____
_____
_____
_____
_____
_____
_____
_____

EMC 3706 • Ancient Egypt •©2003 by Evan-Moor C